# THE STUDENT LAWYER

## HIGH SCHOOL HANDBOOK OF MINNESOTA LAW

Third Edition

**JOSEPH L. DALY**
Professor and Director, Center for Community Legal Education
Hamline University School of Law

with

**JENNIFER D. BLOOM**
Supreme Court Information Office

**EVA P. CAPERTON**
Member, Minnesota State Bar

**LEO M. DALY**
Schwebel, Goetz, Sieben and Hanson, P. A.

**ROGER S. HAYDOCK**
William Mitchell College of Law

**DOUGLAS R. HEIDENREICH**
William Mitchell College of Law

**VIOLET J. SOLLIE**
Member, Minnesota State Bar

**ROGER F. WANGEN**
Minnesota Department of Education

**WEST PUBLISHING COMPANY**
St. Paul    New York    Los Angeles    San Francisco

# CONTENTS

# 7 CONSUMER LAW  105



# 8 ALCOHOL, TOBACCO, DRUGS AND MARIJUANA  135

# 9 LIFESTYLES 149

# EXPLANATION OF CITATIONS

*The Student Lawyer* can be compared to the tip of an enormous iceberg, with the tip being the laws we have covered that pertain most closely to students. The rest of the iceberg would be composed of the many thousands of statutes, case decisions, administrative rulings, and ordinances that have been recorded.

Lawyers must have a general knowledge of the whole "iceberg," though no one lawyer could hope to be proficient in every area of the law. Likewise, no one lawyer or judge can be expected to remember the entire body or even a substantial part of the law specifically. This is why when lawyers argue their cases in court or write down their arguments in statements called *briefs*, they always specify the statutes, cases, or rulings they are relying on, and exactly where they may be found. This is called *citing*. The following are explanations and examples of the citations that have been used in *The Student Lawyer*.

## FEDERAL CITATIONS

*C.F.R.*—Code of Federal Regulations: rules published by various federal agencies enforcing laws of Congress.
*45 C.F.R.* §86.41 means Volume 45, Section 86.41 of the Code of Federal Regulations.

*U.S.C.*—United States Code: the official statutes of the United States.
*29 U.S.C.* §206 means that a specific law may be found in Section 206 of Volume 29 of the United States Code.

*U.S.*—United States Reports: the official record of United States Supreme Court cases.

*Stanley v. Illinois, 405 U.S. 645 (1972)* means that case may be found on page 645 of Volume 405 of United States Reports and was decided in 1972.

*F.2d*—Federal Reporter, Second Series:  the record of Circuit Court of Appeals cases.
*477 F.2d 1292 (8th Cir., 1973)* means Volume 477, page 1292, of the Federal Reporter, Second Series, for the case, which was decided by the Circuit Court of Appeals for the 8th Circuit in 1973.  (Minnesota is one of seven midwestern states in the 8th Circuit).

*Fed. Reg.*—Federal Register: the official "newspaper" for the publication of federal regulations.
*35 Fed. Reg. 11595* means Volume 35, page 11595 of the Federal Register.

*F. Supp.*—Federal Supplement:  the record of Selected Federal District Court cases.
*342 F. Supp. 1224 (D.Minn.1972)* means the volume and page system are the same for the case decided by the Federal District Court for Minnesota in 1972.  (Sometimes this citation is followed by *aff'd 477 F.2d 1292 (8th Cir., 1973)*, which means the case was affirmed by the 8th Circuit Court of Appeals.  In this case, it means that the 8th Circuit agreed with the decision of the Federal District Court of Minnesota.

*P.L.*—Public Law:  the laws passed by Congress that have not yet been recorded in the United States Code.
*PL94-142* refers to the public law from the 94th Congress, the 142nd law passed.  Sometimes even after the public law has been recorded people still refer to the P.L. number.


## MINNESOTA CITATIONS

*Minn.Stat.*—Minnesota Statutes: the official statutes of the state of Minnesota.
*Minn.Stat.* §540.18 means a specific law can be found in Chapter 540, Section 18 of the Minnesota Statutes.

*M.S.A.*—Minnesota Statutes Annotated:  an unofficial compilation of statutes with comments and interpreting cases.
*M.S.A.* §609.07 means a specific law can be found in Chapter 609, Section 07 of the Minnesota Statutes Annotated.

*Minn.*—Minnesota Reports: the official report of Minnesota Supreme Court cases.
*N.W.2d*—Northwestern Reporter, Second Series: unofficial reports of cases decided in several upper midwestern states.  (These two reports are usually cited together.)
*Dellwo v. Pearson, 259 Minn. 452, 107 N.W.2d 859 (1961)* means that case can be found on page 452 of Volume 259 of Minnesota Reports or on page 859 of Volume 107 of the Northwestern Reporter, Second Series, and was decided in 1961.

*Op.Att'y Gen.*—Opinions of the Attorney General: an official collection of selected written opinions of the attorney general, which are requested interpretations of Minnesota law.
*Op.Att'y Gen. 217-F-3 December 15, 1955* means this opinion can be found in the files of Opinions of the Attorney General, file number 217-F-3, for 1955.

*Minn.R.C.P.*—Minnesota Rules of Civil Procedure: the official rules for proceeding with a legal action in the courts of the state of Minnesota.
*Minn.R.C.P. 17.02* means Rule 17, Section 02, of the Minnesota Rules of Civil Procedure.

*Minn.R.Crim.P.*—Minnesota Rules of Criminal Procedure: the official rules for proceeding with a criminal action in the courts of the state of Minnesota.
*Minn.R.Crim.P. 17.06* refers to Rule 17, Section 06, of the Minnesota Rules of Criminal Procedure.

*Minn.J.C.R.*—Minnesota Juvenile Court Rules: the official rules governing all juvenile court proceedings, except in Hennepin and Ramsey Counties, which have their own rules.
*Minn.JCR 5-4* means Rule 5, Section 4, of the Minnesota Juvenile Court Rules.


## LOCAL CITATIONS

*Mpls.Ord.Code*—Minneapolis Code of Ordinances: the official ordinances of the city of Minneapolis.
*Mpls.Ord.Code* §408.050 means a specific ordinance can be found at Chapter 408, Section 050, of the Minneapolis Code of Ordinances.
*St. Paul Leg.Code*—St. Paul Legislative Code: the official ordinances of the city of St. Paul.
*St. Paul Leg.Code* §1045.180 means that a particular ordinance can be found in Section 1045, Subdivision 180, of that collection.

We have attempted to make this book up to date as of the date of publication. However, laws change, and some change very rapidly. It is important that you know there are tools to update the law in these materials for your own research. These tools, called *citators*, are books that list cases or statutes that pertain to or make changes in the case or statute you have looked up. The most famous of the citators is *Shepard's Citators*, a set of books which are so widely used that lawyers call checking their sources for continuing validity and updating *shepardizing*. Shepardizing is fairly easy to learn to do, but you need to have a *Shepard's Citator* in front of you to understand the instructions clearly. Ask your resource person or a law librarian to show you how to do this when you do your research.

# ACKNOWLEDGMENTS

In recognition of their significant contributions, the Minnesota State Bar Association extends its heartfelt appreciation to:

Joseph L. Daly, the chief contributing author and editor-in-chief, without whom this third edition would not exist. His hard work, energy, creativity, and scholarship allowed this book to happen.

The other authors—Jennifer D. Bloom, Eva P. Caperton, Leo M. Daly, Roger S. Haydock, Douglas R. Heidenreich, Violet J. Sollie, and Roger F. Wangen—whose research and writing have greatly helped young people.

Mary Westerman, for her research, citation checking, and beautiful photography, all done while a second-year law student at Hamline University School of Law.

# INTRODUCTION

Many of the nation's leading educators have pointed out that law-related education is being shortchanged because of already-overcrowded curriculums and the emphasis being placed on "back to basics". To vie for students' attention, it seems we would have to come up with something that would motivate and involve them in their own learning experience and, in turn, help develop the values, knowledge, judgments, and skills required for living in and contributing to a democratic society.

Such a goal sounds altruistic, but through our experience gained from compiling material and publishing two previous editions of *The Student Lawyer*, we hope we have learned what is realistic and meaningful to today's student. This third edition has been updated in keeping with law and statute changes. Some chapters have been revised and lengthened, and several new areas of the law have been added. The marginal notes, an innovation in this issue, have been included to stimulate classroom discussions and draw students into the give and take of legal issues.

The authors of *The Student Lawyer*, while dealing with aspects of law that affect students personally, make no attempt to moralize. This might sound like a cop-out when you consider that *The Student Lawyer* was used during a time of student violence and vandalism, teen-age pregnancy and drug abuse, and lack of discipline among youth. But there was a similar mood 200 years age, referred to as the critical period of the 1780's. At that time, however, educators felt that emphasis should be placed on the student as citizen because they believed the common good would win and prevail. Maybe too much faith was being placed in youth, but society did not crumble, nor was the democratic idea discarded for something new.

While memories of the sixties and seventies are still vivid, it seems fitting that the new edition of *The Student Lawyer* continues to project this faith and confidence.  No matter who feels this is misplaced optimism, history would disagree.

Jim Keeler
Director, Communications and Education
Minnesota State Bar Association

# 1

# CIVIL LAW



While criminal laws seek to regulate the conduct of an individual and to provide a punishment for conduct that does not conform to the rules (see Chapter 5 for a discussion of criminal law), the civil law deals with relationships among individuals. If you violate a criminal law you may be arrested, and tried and punished by the state. If you do something that injures your neighbor, you may not have broken a criminal law, but the neighbor may sue you and perhaps recover money damages because of the wrong that you have done.

The injury that you have caused your neighbor may arise out of an intentional or unintentional act. If, for example, you tell lies about someone and an injury results, you may be sued. If you cause someone to receive personal injuries, whether intentionally (as in a fight) or unintentionally (as if you carelessly leave your rake on the sidewalk and someone trips over it), he or she may sue you and recover. These kinds of acts are called *torts*.

Similarly, if you make a binding legal promise and then fail to keep your promise, the person to whom the promise was made may sue you and recover because you have breached your contract. The law governing the creation and enforcement of contracts is complex, but in simple terms we can say that the law establishes formal rules that must be complied with to create a binding contract, and that if a binding contract is created, both parties are expected to live up to it. If one of them does not fulfill the obligations stated in the contract, the law provides a remedy to the other party that, as nearly as possible, puts this party in the same position as if the contract had been performed.

This chapter is designed to tell you something about tort and contract law as they apply to young people. You will see that in some cases young people are treated the same as anyone else and in other cases they are given certain advantages. To round out this brief study of the civil law, the chapter will also touch on property rights of minors, and on wills.

## CASE STUDY

*John, a ten-year-old, borrows a two-week-old ten-speed bike from his neighbor and friend, Fred, who had accidentally broken John's bike. John, just prior to returning Fred's bike, loosens the nuts holding the front wheel. Fred, who has an early morning paper route, is seriously hurt the next day when his front wheel falls off.*

1. What can Fred do? Fred's parents?

2. Who pays the hospital and doctor bills?

3. Who pays for damages to Fred's bike?

4. Has a crime been committed?

5. Can Fred sue? Whom?

---

### SELF-QUIZ

Before you read the chapter, try the following quiz. Answer each question as best you can, based on your general knowledge. When you have read the chapter, go back to see whether or not you have changed your mind about any of the answers. The quiz will not be graded but is here simply to help you discover how much you know about these matters.

1. Minors are liable for their own torts. _______ True _______ False

2. Parents are always responsible for what their children do and must pay if their children damage someone else's property. _______ True _______ False

3. A person will be liable to another person for a commission of a tort only if the hurt to that person was intentional. _______ True _______ False

4. A person under the age of eighteen may sue and recover from another person in a tort action. _______ True _______ False

5. Minors are not allowed to make contracts. _______ True _______ False

6. If an adult enters into a contract with a minor the adult cannot be compelled to fulfill the obligations of the contract. _______ True _______ False

> **7.** Anyone can make a will no matter how old the person is. _____ True _____ False
>
> **8.** A minor may own real property and personal property. _____ True _____ False
>
> **9.** If the owner of a car lends it to a friend and the friend has an accident, the owner is liable to the injured party. _____ True _____ False
>
> **10.** A minor who enters into a contract can call it off before becoming an adult. _____ True _____ False

*What is civil law?*

Civil law is the opposite of criminal law in that it deals with private rights. Under the criminal law, the state takes a person to court and asks that this person be punished by fine or imprisonment for an act harmful to society. The civil law involves one person taking another to court to settle a dispute between them. Usually the person who sues asks for **damages** (the payment of money) from the other. Sometimes one person will ask for the court to prohibit the other person from doing something—this is called an *injunction*. The person asking for relief is called the **plaintiff**; the person sued is called the **defendant**.

**damages:** money received for injuries or losses suffered.

**plaintiff:** the person who starts a legal action against another person.

**defendant:** the person against whom a legal action is brought.

| CIVIL CASE | CRIMINAL CASE |
|---|---|
| *Rodriguez v. Chan* | *State of Minnesota v. Nelson* |
| (Plaintiff vs. Defendant) | (Prosecutor vs. Defendant) |
| Penalty: Damages | Penalty: Jail and/or fine |

## TORTS

*What is a tort?*

A **tort** is an injury to a person or damage to someone's property that is caused by another person's acts. There are four main kinds of torts: intentional (torts arising from injury done on purpose), negligent (torts arising from carelessness), strict liability (torts arising out of defects in certain products), and liability without fault (torts arising from conduct that, by its very nature, creates a high degree of risk). A person who commits a tort can be sued and may have to pay for the damage caused.

**tort:** an injury caused by another person's act.

KINDS OF TORTS
intentional
negligent
strict liability
liability without fault

*Can a minor be sued for a tort?*

Yes. Even small children can be sued for their torts. Being underage does not allow one to hurt other people. (*Johanson v. Lunda*, 157 Minn. 260, 195 N.W.

917 (1923))  The person you hurt could get a judgment against you and wait to collect until you are older and have some money and property.  A judgment is an official court paper that says that you have lost a lawsuit and that the person who won is entitled to receive a certain amount of money from you.  Judgments are renewable and can be kept active for many years.

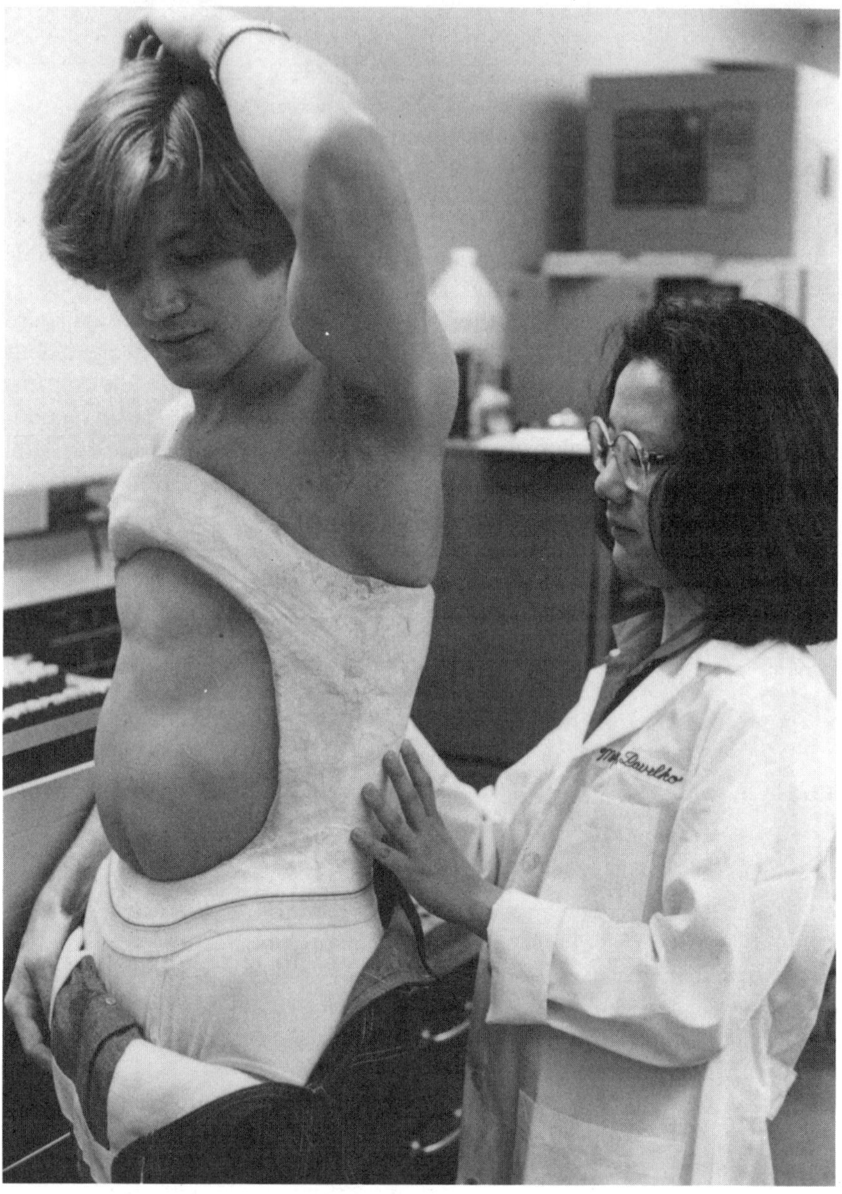

*Intentional torts can result in serious medical problems.*

*What kinds of things might be torts?*

*Liability without fault* is uncommon and it is unlikely that you would do anything that would result in this, although it might apply if you were using dynamite or some other explosive. If you do that, you could be liable for damages to anyone who was hurt even though you were very careful and could not have avoided hurting that person.

    *Strict liability* is also uncommon and arises in the case of the production of goods for use by the general public. Liability arises if damages are incurred as a result of a defect in a product which, by its own terms, would be inherently dangerous if defective. (*McCormack v. Hankscraft Co.*, 278 Minn. 322, 154 N.W. 2d 488 (1967))

    You are not likely to commit an *intentional tort* either. The most common of these are assault (hurting somebody in a fight or deliberately injuring someone in some other way), fraud (deliberately lying to someone to cheat him or her), and libel or slander (telling lies about someone and hurting that person's reputation).

    *Negligent torts* are more common. There are many ways to hurt someone through carelessness, but one of the most common is the automobile accident. If you drive a car or other motor vehicle carelessly and cause an accident, you may be liable. It is obviously **negligent** to drive while you are intoxicated, to speed, to drive on the wrong side of the road, or to run a red light. In other cases, whether or not you were careless depends on the specific facts; if you are sued, a jury would decide whether or not you were careless. In Minnesota and in some other states an injured person can't recover from a negligent person for small losses in auto accident cases. The "no-fault" law says that the injured person's economic loss must be recovered from his or her own insurance company. (M.S.A. 65B.41 thru 65B.71) The most controversial portion of the no-fault act has been its taking from innocent accident victims the right to pursue a claim for pain, suffering, and disability against the negligent motorist, except in cases of rather serious injury.

**negligent:** careless

$$\left.\begin{array}{l}\text{Duty} \\ \text{Breach of Duty}\end{array}\right\} \quad \text{Negligence}$$

$$\downarrow$$

$$\text{Proximate Cause}$$

$$\downarrow$$

$$\text{Damages}$$

*Are minors treated differently than adults?*

There are two major differences when a minor is sued for a tort. First, no minor can go to court without a **guardian ad litem**—this is a special legal term that refers to an adult appointed by the court to represent the minor at the time of the trial. The guardian works with the minor's lawyer to protect his or her interests and usually has the power to make the decisions about how the lawsuit is to be handled. Usually the guardian is a parent of the minor, although any other adult can serve as guardian. If you need a guardian, you

**guardian ad litem:** an adult appointed by a court to represent a minor.

*Accidents are one kind of tort.*

can go to court and ask the court to appoint one for you. (Minn.R.C.P. 17.02) Second, in deciding whether or not a minor has been negligent, the law compares his or her acts with those of a reasonably careful adult. Normally the minor's more limited experience is taken into account and he or she is not required to act as quickly or as well as an older person who has more experience. However, a minor who operates an automobile, airplane, or boat loses this special protection. The law says that when minors use these dangerous machines they must act as reasonably careful adults would in the same circumstances. (*Dellwo v. Pearson*, 259 Minn. 452, 107 N.W. 2d 859 (1961))

*Can a minor sue another person for a tort?*

Yes. However, again you must have a guardian, and if you have medical bills, your parents must sue to collect the bills since they are liable to pay them. (Minn. Stat. §540.08) Your parent or guardian ad litem may settle the suit for you if the other side offers to pay you some money without going to court. However, the law requires the judge's approval of a settlement so that you will be protected. (Minn. Stat. §540.08)

*Do my parents have to pay for damages caused by my torts?*

Usually no person has to pay for the torts of another person, but there are some exceptions. Your parents can be required to pay for any malicious damage you do to a person or to property, if you are living at home and under eighteen, but the most that they will have to pay is $500. (Minn. Stat. §540.18) You could still be sued to pay for the rest of the bills if the damage was greater than $500. If you cause an accident with your parents' car, they will be liable for the damage you cause. This is not because they are your parents, but because they are responsible for the acts of *anyone* who borrows their car with their permission.   (Minn. Stat. §170.54) You would still be liable too, and both you and your parents could be sued. Again, some accidents will be covered by the no-fault statute (see Chapter 9).

*Does this mean that if I borrow a friend's car, he or she is liable for what I do?*

Yes. The rule also applies if you use your employer's car while on the job. It also means that you should be careful about lending your own car to other people, because you can be forced to pay for the damage they cause.

*Can a bar that sells me liquor be forced to pay for my accident?*

Yes. The Civil Damages Act (sometimes called the Dram Shop Law) says that if anyone sells or gives liquor to another person illegally and that person becomes intoxicated and causes an accident, the one who provided the liquor can be liable. (Minn. Stat. §340.95) The Minnesota Supreme Court has said this statute also means that a person who serves you liquor at a private party can be responsible, if the liquor was given to you illegally. (*Ross v. Ross*, 294 Minn. 115, 200 N.W. 2d 149 (1972))

In 1977 the legislature amended Minn. Stat. 340.95 and said liability only results if an illegal "selling and bartering" has taken place. Some people argue that this means that the legislature has changed the ruling of the Minnesota Supreme Court so that the law no longer holds the "host" of the party liable. The amendment has not yet been decided in court.

> Legislative → Legislature → makes the laws
>
> Judicial → Supreme Court → interprets the laws
>
> Executive → Governor → enforces the laws

*Is it true that being sued for a tort can ruin me and my family for life?*

It is possible but not very likely. However, if you injure someone badly or cause the death of a breadwinner, the loss to this person's family can be very large. Since most people cannot afford to pay the damages arising for causing such injuries, they protect themselves with liability insurance. This kind of insurance pays the person you injured whenever you would be responsible to pay. Nearly everybody has automobile accident liability insurance, and most people have homeowner's insurance to protect the members of the family from other kinds of negligent torts. (If, for example, you carelessly hit a baseball into the pitcher's head, your parents' homeowner's insurance might pay for the damages.) There is no insurance you can buy that will insure against your liability for an intentional tort, so if you deliberately hurt somebody, you might have to pay a great deal of money from your own pocket.

## CONTRACTS

*What is a contract?*

contract: a legally
enforceable agreement
between two or more
people.

A **contract** is an agreement that a court will enforce in a lawsuit. It does not have to be written, but if it is oral it will be harder to prove the contract was made. Each person must give something of value to the other person or promise to give something of value before a contract exists. A person who breaks the agreement can be sued and might have to pay damages to the other person so that that person will be as well off as if the agreement had been carried out. Courts may refuse to enforce contracts secured by force or fraud, or entered into by incompetent persons.

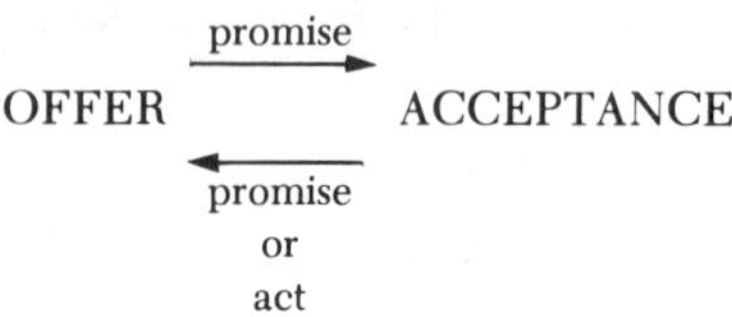


*Is it true that minors can't make contracts?*

This is not exactly true. Minors can make contracts, but the contract of a minor is voidable at the minor's option. This means that the minor can refuse to go through with the agreement and cannot be forced to pay damages. (*Nichols & Shephard Co. v. Snyder*, 78 Minn. 502, 81 N.W. 516 (1900)) Even if the contract in the case of a purchase has been carried out, a minor may decide while still a minor, or within a reasonable time after becoming of age,

**WHAT
DO
YOU
THINK?**

Pierre, age seventeen, got a job through ABC employment agency. He signed a contract with ABC saying he would give them thirty percent of his first ten paychecks. Does Pierre have to pay ABC? Why or why not? Should Pierre have to give up his job if he doesn't want to pay? Do minors need special protection when making contracts? Why? How old should people be before they can make contracts? Why?

*Know the terms of a contract before signing it.*

to undo the contract and get his or her money back.  (*Kelly v. Furlong*, 194 Minn. 465, 261 N.W. 460 (1935))

*Can a minor ever be forced to go through with a contract?*

Yes.  A minor can be required to pay a reasonable price under a contract to purchase necessities (the things that are needed to live in a normal and moderate manner).  (*Miller v. Smith*, 26 Minn. 248, 2 N.W. 942 (1879)) (Although the Minnesota Supreme Court has never had to decide the question, most other courts that have heard such cases have decided that a car is *not* a necessity.)

*Does this mean I can buy a car, keep it, and get my money back by voiding the contract?*

No.  In order to recover your money, you must return the property if you still have it.  Even if the car has been wrecked, you probably will still be able to void the contract, but in Minnesota you will probably have to account to the seller for such benefit as you may have received from having the car in your possession.

*What happens if I lie about my age so that someone will make a contract with me?*

This makes no difference; the contract is still **voidable** because of the inexperience of minors in understanding the nature and propriety of contracts they may make. (*Conrad v. Lane*, 26 Minn. 389, 4 N.W. 695 (1880))

**voidable:** valid but can be declared invalid (a contract between an adult and a minor).

*Can an adult who contracts with me refuse to go through with the contract?*

No.  A minor's contracts are voidable at the minor's election.  This means that they bind any adult who agrees to them.

**void:** absolutely invalid (a contract to murder someone).

## PROPERTY RIGHTS

*Can a minor own property?*

Yes.  However, if the property owned is substantial or valuable, the minor normally cannot use it or decide how it will be used.  Normally property owned by a minor is "in trust."  This means that the money is managed by a "trustee"—a person or bank that is required to protect the property and use it for the minor's best interests.  A trust will sometimes have very specific rules about how the property is to be used, and usually the minor will get complete control of the property on becoming eighteen years old.  (M.S.A. 168.101 subd. 1)

*Why can't minors manage their own money?*

Usually any property a minor owns has been left to him or her by relatives at their death, or given to him or her by a family member.  (Normally a minor does have control, at least as a practical matter, over money earned or personal items owned.) However, the law believes that minors do not have the experience to manage large sums of money or valuable property. Wills of parents or other relatives are often written to put the property in trust. If there is no will, a court will appoint a guardian of the minor's property. (Minn. Stat. §§525.56 and 525.504) Minnesota also has a Uniform Gifts to Minors Act, which sets up a detailed system to make it easier for an adult to give stocks and bonds or life insurance policies to a minor. The statute requires that a custodian (similar to a trustee) be appointed to manage the property. (Minn. Stat. §527)

## WILLS

*What if my father dies without a will?*

**intestate succession:** dying without a will.

The process by which property is distributed when there is no will is called **intestate succession.** If your father dies without a will, you are entitled to a share of all his property. The size of the share depends on whether or not your mother is still alive and how many brothers and sisters you have. In general, your mother would get at least one-third and you and your brothers and sisters would divide up the rest. Property would be distributed in the same way if your mother died. (Minn. Stat. §525.16) A husband cannot cut his wife out of his will, nor can a wife disinherit her husband. (Minn. Stat. §525.16) A parent can disinherit a child, however, because the law does not forbid it. However, a child normally has some interest in the "homestead" (the family home) and is protected by the parents' duty to support. (Minn. Stat. §525.145) See also Chapter 3, Parents and Children.

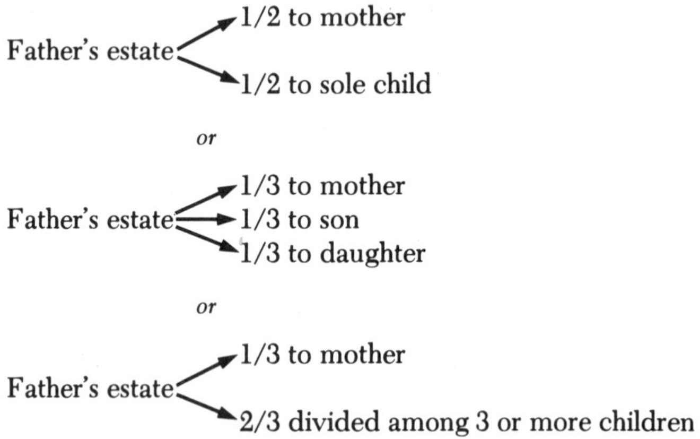


*Can a minor make a will?*

No.   (Minn. Stat. §525.18)

*Who gets a minor's property when he or she dies?*

Any property that you inherited from one of your parents would go to any other children that parent had, or grandchildren or other descendants of that parent. Other property, in the case of an unmarried minor, goes to the minor's parents if they are living, and if not, then to the minor's brothers and sisters or, if there are none, to some other more distant relative. (Minn. Stat. §525.16) If an unmarried minor had a child, this property would go to the child. (Minn. Stat. §525.172)


## PROBLEM 1

John is a high school student, seventeen years of age, who looks much older. One day he goes to Friendly Fred's Used Car Lot and buys an automobile, paying Fred $700 in cash. John drives the car for a couple of weeks and all goes well until he loans the car to William, a sixteen-year-old friend.

William, who looks considerably older than his age, goes to a bar where he is served enough liquor to make him drunk. He leaves the bar, gets into John's car, and before he has driven a block, has an accident in which Carl, the driver of the other car, is seriously injured. John's car is totally demolished but, miraculously, William is unhurt. John has the car towed to Friendly Fred's lot. He wants to return the car, saying that he wishes to void his contract, and he asks for the return of his $700. Fred refuses to return the money.

Consider the following questions:

1. If John sues Fred to recover his $700, will he be successful? Why or why not?

2. Whom may Carl sue? Will he be able to recover from any of those that he sues? If so, why? If not, why not?

Now that you have thought about these problems go back to the quiz at the beginning of the chapter and see whether or not you will change your mind about any of your answers. Feel free to consult the text material in this chapter for assistance.

# 2

# MARRIAGE

## CONTENTS



Marriage is a serious undertaking. Marriage gives rise to many legal obligations and rights that are enforceable in a court of law. These rights and obligations are of concern not only to the person directly involved, but to the people of the state of Minnesota as well. Accordingly, the state has established rules closely governing the process of marrying and dissolving marriages, and the rights of the parties during the marriage relationship.

The material in this chapter is designed to explain the technical rules involved in obtaining a marriage license and getting married. It will also explain some of the duties and responsibilities that married partners undertake.

## CASE STUDY

*Sally, age sixteen, and Ralph, age sixteen, after going steady for one year, decide to get married during the Christmas holidays. Neither could get their parents' approval but both have identification showing each to be eighteen.*

*They decide to go to Iowa to get married because it is easier there. They ask you for some help and advice, including being a witness for their marriage.*

1. What are you going to do?

2. What are some of their problems with the Minnesota law?

3. If they are married, is the marriage legal?

---

**SELF-QUIZ**

Before you read the chapter, try the following quiz. Answer each question as best you can, based on your general knowledge. When you have read the chapter, go back to see whether or not you have changed your mind about any of the answers.

1. Both parties must be at least eighteen years old in order to marry. _______ True _______ False

2. Marriage emancipates the parties, and they are no longer subject to the control of their parents for most purposes. _______ True _______ False

3. A marriage entered into in another state is not valid if it does not meet the requirements of the state where the parties really live. _______ True _______ False

4. Only a minister, priest, or rabbi can perform a binding marriage ceremony. _______ True _______ False

5. There is a five-day waiting period between the time of application for a marriage license and issuance of the license in Minnesota. _______ True _______ False

6. A marriage between first cousins is void in Minnesota. _______ True _______ False

7. A high school may expel a student who gets married. _______ True _______ False

8. After marriage each spouse has the legal authority to bind the other spouse to any contract agreement made with other people. _______ True _______ False

9. The husband has the legal obligation to support his wife. _______ True _______ False

10. A married couple separate but do not petition to dissolve the marriage. Later the wife inherits some real property and decides to sell. The husband can prevent this sale. _______ True _______ False

11. A girl marries at sixteen with the consent of her parents and the juvenile court. She thereby gains all the rights of an adult. _______ True _______ False

---

## AGE AND CONSENT

*When can I get married?*

1. If you are eighteen years of age or older, you can get married without your parents' consent whether you are a boy or a girl.

**2.** If you are a boy or a girl age sixteen or seventeen, you may marry if you have either the written consent of your parents or the consent of the juvenile court judge for your county. Before your application for a marriage license is approved, the juvenile court judge may ask you why you want to get married. Your application can be refused if the judge feels your reasons for marriage are not good ones.

**3.** If you are a boy or girl younger than sixteen, you may marry if you have the written consent of your parents and the consent of the juvenile court judge for your county. (Minn. Stat. §517.02)

*What can happen if we lie about our ages to get married?*

**1.** If either of you could not be married at all, the marriage is absolutely void. The law will treat you as if you had never gone through a marriage ceremony. It is not necessary to end the marriage by petitioning the court to obtain a dissolution or annulment because in the eyes of the law there was no marriage. (Minn. Stat. §518.01)

**2.** If you were married without the consent of your parents or a juvenile court judge and consent was necessary, the marriage is voidable. This means that the person who was underage at the time of the marriage may go to court and have the marriage ended by annulment. (Minn. Stat. §518.02) The marriage cannot be annulled if the parties lived together as husband and wife

*A couple under eighteen must get permission to marry.*

after they both reached the age of consent. In this case, a dissolution must be sought. (Minn. Stat. §518.04)

3. Lying under oath is called perjury and is a very serious crime. If you lie to the clerk of court about your age after having sworn to tell the truth, you might be prosecuted or declared delinquent as a result. (Minn. Stat. §609.48)

## LICENSE

*How do I get a marriage license?*

You must apply for the license from the clerk of the district court of the county. (This office is normally found in the county courthouse.) You must tell the clerk under oath your names, addresses, ages, social security numbers, whether or not you are related to each other, the name and address of a person's parents if that person is under eighteen, and if you have ever been married before. You must then wait five days to get the license. The clerk may refuse to give you a license if you are already married or if you are applying to marry a relative closer than a second cousin, or if you are incompetent. (Minn. Stat. §517.08)

## MARRIAGE CEREMONY

*Who can perform a marriage ceremony?*

Any judge or licensed or ordained minister may perform a marriage. In some cases the residential school administrators of the Minnesota School for the Deaf and the Minnesota Braille and Sight-Saving School may also perform marriages. (Minn. Stat. §517.04)

*If I go to another state to get married, will that marriage be recognized in Minnesota?*

There is a general rule of law, recognized in Minnesota, that if the marriage is valid under the laws of the state in which it is performed, it is valid everywhere. (*In re Kinkead's Estate*, 239 Minn. 27, 57 N.W.2d 628 (1953)) Note that the marriage first has to be valid in the state where it is performed. For example, an Ohio marriage is recognized as valid in Minnesota if it was valid under Ohio law when performed there.

## LEGAL OBLIGATIONS

*What legal obligations result from a valid marriage?*

Marriage is a kind of contract. That means that each of the two people involved has certain duties toward the other partner. The state has an interest in this kind of contract and the partners cannot decide to end the marriage unless the state agrees and dissolves the marriage. (*Gerber v. Gerber*, 241 Minn. 346, 64 N.W.2d 779 (1954)) The husband has a duty to support his wife and children, and to pay for their necessities. The wife is primarily liable for her own necessities; if she cannot provide those personal needs, her husband is responsible for supporting her. (*Busch v. General Motors*, 262 N.W.2d 377 (1978)) Even if the marriage is dissolved, the husband must continue to support his children and he may have to provide for his former wife through spousal maintenance or property division. (Minn. Stat. §§ 518.55, .552 and .57; *Messer v. Messer*, 289 Minn. 449, 184 N.W.2d 801 (1971))

*Do I have to pay all of my husband's or wife's bills?*

Not always. The husband must pay the wife's creditors (people she owes money to) for necessities if she does not pay for them. He would pay for the same things he would have to buy her if he was supporting her directly. Both the husband and wife, if they are living together, can be sued for all things either of them bought for their home. (Minn. Stat. §519.05) See the section on contracts in Chapter 1.

*How many children are born out of wedlock in Minnesota?*

**FIGURE 2-1  Application for Marriage License**

CDC-846

| BOOK | PAGE |
|---|---|
| | |

STATE OF MINNESOTA
County of ______Ramsey______ } ss
Fee: $15.00

## APPLICATION FOR MARRIAGE LICENSE
(Please Print)

**GROOM**

| NAME (First) | (Middle) | (Last) | Number of previous marriages |
|---|---|---|---|
| ADDRESS (Number and street) | | PHONE # WORK/HOME | How last marriage terminated<br>Death ☐ Divorce ☐ Annulment ☐ |
| CITY OR TOWNSHIP | COUNTY | STATE | Date terminated |
| AGE / BIRTHDATE | BIRTHPLACE (state or foreign country) / RACE | | Place of termination |
| PREVIOUS MARRIED NAME (First) | (Middle) | (Last) | Court where terminated |

**BRIDE**

| NAME (First) | (Middle) | (Last) | Number of previous marriages |
|---|---|---|---|
| ADDRESS (Number and street) | | PHONE # WORK/HOME | How last marriage terminated<br>Death ☐ Divorce ☐ Annulment ☐ |
| CITY OR TOWNSHIP | COUNTY | STATE | Date Terminated |
| AGE / BIRTHDATE | BIRTHPLACE (state or foreign country) / RACE | | Place of termination |
| PREVIOUS MARRIED NAME (First) | (Middle) | (Last) | Court where terminated |

| If the bride is under 18 years of age, give the name and address of her parents or guardian. | NAME |
|---|---|
| | ADDRESS |

| Are the parties related to each other by blood or adoption?<br>Yes ☐   No ☐ | If yes, what is the relationship? | |
|---|---|---|
| Give the name and date of birth of any child-(ren) of which _both_ parties are the parents, unless the parental rights have been terminated. | NAME | DATE OF BIRTH |

| Give the names the parties will have after marriage: | GROOM'S NAME (First) / (Middle) / (Last) |
|---|---|
| | BRIDE'S NAME (First) / (Middle) / (Last) |

| Address the parties will have after marriage: | ADDRESS (Number and street) |
|---|---|
| | CITY / STATE / ZIP |

I, We, the undersigned, hereby apply for a license to marry _________________________________ ,
and declare upon oath that all the above answers and statements of fact are true and correct; that neither of us has a spouse living; that neither of us is a mentally deficient person committed to the guardianship or conservatorship of the commissioner of public welfare, and that one of the applicants is a man and the other is a woman.

Signatures  X_____________________
X_____________________

Subscribed and sworn to before me this _________ day of _________________ , 19_____

______J.E. GOCKOWSKI______   By_____________________
Clerk of the District Court            (Deputy)

MARRIAGE DATE SET FOR: _____________________

**OFFICE USE ONLY**

DATE LICENSE ISSUED

PLACE OF MARRIAGE

DATE OF MARRIAGE

TYPE OF CEREMONY
CIVIL ☐   RELIGIOUS ☐

Application form provided courtesy of Clerk of Court, Ramsey County

**TABLE 2-1   Laws and Rules that Relate to Marriage in the State of Minnesota**

<u>WHERE TO APPLY:</u>

Either or both parties to the proposed marriage must apply before the clerk of district court, in person, to make application for a marriage license.

<u>RESIDENCE:   (Amended)</u>
M.S.A.   517.07

The license may be obtained from the clerk of district court in any county within the state.  The marriage need not take place in the county where the license was obtained.

<u>AGE:</u>
M.S.A.   517.02

A male or female must be 18 years to marry without consent of parents.  If 16, the consent of both parents, if living, must be given on behalf of the minor, in writing and sworn to before a notary public.  Or consent to the marriage may be obtained from the juvenile court in the county in which he or she resides.  A minor under 16 years of age may marry if he or she has written consent of both parents, if living, and the consent of the juvenile court.

<u>PROOF OF</u>
<u>AGE:</u>

Applicants under the age of 21 years are required to produce a birth certificate or some other proof of age.

<u>CONSENT OF DIVORCED</u>
<u>PARENT:</u>

A divorced parent giving consent to a marriage of a minor child must present a certified copy of the divorce decree or other court order granting custody of the minor child.

<u>APPLICATION FOR</u>
<u>LICENSE:  (Amended)</u>
M.S.A.   517.08

If either party has previously been married, his or her married name, and the date, place, and court in which the marriage was dissolved or annulled or the date and place of death of the former spouse must be supplied.  If either party is a minor, the name and address of the minor's parents or guardian must be furnished.  It must be established whether the parties are related to each other, and, if so, what their relationship is.

Applicants must supply the name and date of birth of any child (of which both parties are parents) born before the making of the application, unless their parental rights have been terminated.

<u>PROHIBITED</u>
<u>MARRIAGES:  (Amended)</u>
M.S.A.   517.03

a. A marriage entered prior to the dissolution of an earlier marriage of one of the parties;
b. A marriage between an ancestor and a descendant, or brother and sister, whether the relationship is by half or whole blood or by adoption;
c. A marriage between an uncle and a niece, between an aunt and a nephew, or between first cousins, whether the relationship is by the half or the whole blood, except as to marriages permitted by the established customs of aboriginal cultures;
d. Mentally deficient persons committed to the guardianship of the Commissioner of Public Welfare and mentally deficient persons committed to the conservatorship of the Commissioner of Public Welfare in which the terms of the conservatorship limit the right to marry, may marry with the consent of the commissioner.  The

**TABLE 2-1——**—*Continued*

|  |  |
|---|---|
|  | clerk of the district court shall not issue a license unless he has received a signed copy of the consent of the Commissioner of Public Welfare. |
| WAITING PERIOD<br>AND FEE:<br>M.S.A. 517.08 | Application for a marriage license shall be made at least five days before a license shall be issued.  The clerk shall collect from the applicant a fee of $30.  This waiting period may be waived through an order of the court. |
| DIVORCE: | Effective March 1, 1979, there is no longer any waiting period before a couple can apply for a marriage license, regardless of when either party may have been granted a divorce. However, the clerk of district court will still require proof that the dissolution was granted. |

Courtesy of Clerk of Court, Ramsey County


## EMANCIPATION BY MARRIAGE

*Do I become emancipated when I legally marry?*

**emancipation:** complete parental surrender of care, custody, and earnings of a child.

**Emancipation** is the ending of legal ties between parent and child.  It can be complete or partial.  Emancipation occurs automatically when you become eighteen, and it may occur earlier.

One of the ways emancipation can occur before you reach the age of consent (eighteen) is through marriage.  This emancipation is not complete. While your parents or a guardian would no longer have the right to control your activities, they would have the right to control substantial or valuable property as guardians of your welfare. (Minn. Stat. §525.60) For example, a girl of sixteen who is legally married to an eighteen-year-old would not have to account to her parents or guardian for her hours, or to secure their permission to change her residence; nor could she claim support from such sources as social security or worker's compensation that she was collecting as a dependent of her parents.  (Minn. Stat. §176.111)  However, if she has inherited or been given substantial valuable property, her parents or guardian would still hold the property in trust (controlling it for her benefit) until she reaches the age of consent or another age specified for her control of the property.


## PROBLEM 1

Helen and Herbert, both seventeen years of age, obtained a marriage license with falsified birth certificates.  They were married and rented an apartment.  Herbert and Helen both worked and they lived comfortably until Helen became ill and incurred substantial medical bills.

As money became tighter and tighter Herbert couldn't pay the rent on the apartment and couldn't pay the medical bills.  The couple moved to the home of some friends where they could stay rent-free.  The owner of the apartment is claiming eight months' rent for the balance of the term of a lease that both Helen and Herbert signed when they moved into the apartment.

Helen's parents had "washed their hands of her" when she married Herbert and wanted nothing to do with her.  Herbert has now left Helen and is living with some friends.  Helen is pregnant.  Both Helen and Herbert are now eighteen years of age.

1.  Is the marriage void?  Voidable?  Completely valid?

2.  Does the landlord have any valid claim against Helen or Herbert for rent?

3.  Does Helen have any claim against her parents for her medical expenses?

4.  What are Herbert's obligations to Helen?

5.  Has Herbert committed any crimes?



## PROBLEM 2

John, age eighteen, and Jane, age sixteen, have decided to get married.  They visit their local marriage bureau, are told to fill out the marriage license application (see the application reproduced earlier in this chapter), and are then interviewed by a clerk.

1.  What questions might they expect the clerk to ask?

2.  Why are each of the questions included on the marriage license application?

# 3

# PARENTS AND CHILDREN

## CONTENTS



For the first eighteen years or more of your life you will probably live with your parents. When you are young they will provide food and clothing and a place for you to live, but as you grow older you may assume some of these responsibilities yourself. If you become a parent, you will have the same responsibilities as an adult parent, irrespective of your age.

The relationship between parents and children is a very special one, subject to many rules of both statutory and case law. Each has certain obligations toward the other; however, the state also has an interest in protecting young people, particularly children who are unable to protect themselves. Therefore, if parents fail to discharge their responsibilities to their children, the state may step in and go so far as to remove the children from their parents' custody, if that seems best for the child.

The material in this chapter is designed to point out some of the problems that arise out of the parent-child relationship, and to suggest ways that the law deals with these problems. Before you read the material in the chapter, answer the following true-false questions to see whether or not your ideas about these topics are accurate.

## CASE STUDY

*Mary, a sixteen-year-old, has a year-round job that permits her to work only part-time when school is in session. When her parents insist she pay part of her wages for board and room at home, she and her parents have a fight. As a result, she leaves home with a seriously bruised arm and moves in with an older girl.*

1. What responsibilities do her parents have for providing board and room?

2. If Mary's parents call the police, can the police force her to return home?

3. Do her parents have any legal right to Mary's wages?

---

**SELF-QUIZ**

---

Before you read the chapter, try the following quiz. Answer each question as best you can, based on your general knowledge. When you have read the chapter, go back to see whether or not you have changed your mind about any of the answers.

1. A child who earns money at a job may retain the earnings and does not have to give any money to his or her parents. _______ True _______ False

2. Parents may spank a child for misbehaving. _______ True _______ False

3. A child who runs away from home cannot be brought back from another state. _______ True _______ False

4. Parents must always give their consent if their child receives medical treatment. _______ True _______ False

5. If a child goes to a doctor for a venereal disease (V.D.) test, the doctor is required by law to disclose the results to the parents. _______ True _______ False

6. Parents are required to provide only bare minimum amounts of food and clothing for their children. _______ True _______ False

7. If parents do not support their children, the only consequence is that the children may be taken from them. _______ True _______ False

8. Children have no obligation whatsoever to their parents. _______ True _______ False

9. A child is automatically emancipated on becoming sixteen years old. _______ True _______ False

10. The father of an illegitimate child must pay for the support and education of the child until it is an adult, even though the mother marries someone else later. _______ True _______ False

11. An unmarried father never has a legal right to get custody of his illegitimate child. _______ True _______ False

12. If you are eighteen years old, your parents have no legal right to control you. _______ True _______ False

13. Parents have absolute control over their minor children, and the government can never interfere with this. _______ True _______ False

14. A doctor is required by law to report cases of child abuse to the local welfare agency. _______ True _______ False

**15.** Parents' obligations toward their children can vary, depending on the age of the children. _______ True _______ False
**16.** A stepparent can never physically punish a child because it is not "really" his or her child.  _______ True _______ False
**17.** Parents have unlimited authority over how to discipline their children. _______ True _______ False
**18.** Children can be removed from their parents' custody if a judge believes that the parents cannot properly care for their children.  _______ True _______ False

## SUPPORT AND EDUCATION

*What does my parents' duty to support me mean?*

In general, they must provide you with necessary shelter, food, medical care, and education.  Of course, they don't have to buy you anything that is very expensive; they simply have to give you those things that you really need and that they can afford to provide.  (Minn. Stat. §260.221)

*What does my parents' duty to educate and protect me mean?*

This does not just mean that they must send you to school, but also that they must provide you with normal parental attention, care, and instruction.  The amount of care a parent must give depends on the age of the child; naturally, a small child requires more attention than a teenager.  However, the parents of a teenager must provide some care and must not create an atmosphere that is detrimental to the physical, mental, or moral health of their children. (Minn. Stat. §260.221)

*What will happen if my parents don't do these things?*

If your parents fail to support you when they can afford to do so, if they abandon you, if they fail to care for you and protect you, or if they create an unhealthy or immoral atmosphere in your home, the juvenile court can terminate your parents' rights and take custody away from them.  (Minn. Stat. §260.221)  The juvenile court could say that you were "neglected" or "dependent" and:

**1.** leave you in your own home under the supervision of the county welfare board or a child placement agency, or

**2.** transfer legal custody to a child placement agency or the county welfare board, or

**3.** order your parents to provide any special care or treatment you may need.  (Minn. Stat. §260.191)

*Parents have a duty to educate, care for, and protect their children.*

*Can my parents be arrested if they don't support me?*

If you are under sixteen and are needy and if your parents can afford to support you and intentionally fail to do so, they may be guilty of a *misdemeanor*: punishable by ninety days in jail or a fine of $300. If the nonsupport continues for more than ninety days, the parent is guilty of a *felony* and could be put in prison for five years. (Minn. Stat. §609.375)

## OBEDIENCE

*Do I have to obey my parents?*

Yes. If you are under eighteen and if your parents can't control you or you are habitually disobedient, the juvenile court could say that you are a "delinquent child." (Minn. Stat. §260.015)  This might mean that the judge would simply counsel you and your parents.  But if the judge thought it was necessary, you could be put under the supervision of a probation officer; or custody could be transferred to a child placement agency, the county welfare board, a county home school, a foster home, or the Minnesota Corrections Authority.  (Minn. Stat. §260.191)

## EARNINGS

*If I have a job do my parents have a right to my earnings?*

Yes.  Your parents are entitled to your "services" because they support you.  (*Grosovsky v. Goldenberg*, 86 Minn. 278, 90 N.W. 782 (1902))  However, your parents must notify the employer that they are claiming a right to your salary.  If they fail to notify your employer, the payment to you is valid.  (Minn. Stat. §181.01)

If money has been left to you by will or given to you as a gift, your parents cannot take it.  Sometimes this kind of gift is set up so that your parents can use some of it for your support or education, if necessary.

## PHYSICAL PUNISHMENT

*Can my parents hit me or punish me physically if I don't obey them?*

Yes.  Parents may use reasonable force to "restrain" or "correct" a child in the exercise of their lawful authority over the child.  (Minn. Stat. §609.06)

*What does this mean?*

The statute apparently applies to any person under eighteen years of age or to any high school pupil.  (Pirsig, Comment, M.S.A. §609.06)  It not only applies to parents and legal guardians, but also allows stepparents to use physical punishment if they have supported the child and treated him or her as a member of the family. (*State v. Weber*, 272 Minn. 243, 137 N.W.2d 527 (1965))

*How much force can my parents use?*

"Reasonable force" does not include so much force that you would be severely injured.  The Minnesota Supreme Court has said that more than reasonable force was used when a stepfather punished a boy so severely that he caused cuts, bruises, and a concussion.  (*State v. Weber*, 272 Minn. 243, 137 N.W.2d 527 (1965))  If your parents really injure you they may be guilty of assault (a misdemeanor) or aggravated assault (a felony), depending on how badly you are hurt.  (Minn. Stat. §§609.22 and .225)

---

**WHAT
DO
YOU
THINK?**

Is there a difference between corporal punishment and child abuse?  Can a child be abused without being hit? What damages do you see in child abuse?  How will an abused child likely be as an adult?

## CHILD ABUSE

*What should I do if I suspect that a friend of mine is being physically abused by his or her parents?*

**child abuse:** repeated or multiple trauma (injury), whether physical or psychological, or a major trauma.

The Minnesota Legislature passed a law in 1975 concerning **child abuse.** (See Minn. Stat. §626.555)  The law expresses a public policy to protect the neglected or abused child.  It requires certain individuals (teachers, doctors, police officers, and social workers) to report to their local welfare agency cases of child abuse.  Although you, as students, are not required to report these cases, it may be a good idea to tell a school official if you sincerely believe that a classmate or friend of yours is being abused or neglected by his or her parents.

## NEGLECTED OR DEPENDENT CHILDREN

*What are neglected children?*

Neglected children are people who are under eighteen and who have been *abandoned by their parents*; who are without proper care because of the way their parents treat them; who are without necessary food, shelter, education, or other care because *their parents fail to provide it*; whose behavior, condition, job, or associates are dangerous to themselves or others; or whose conduct is the same as that of delinquent children but is caused by their *parents' neglect.*  (Minn. Stat. §260.015(20))

*What are dependent children?*

Ten percent of all children in the United States receive Aid to Families with Dependent Children (AFDC) benefits.  In 1980 the federal government spent almost $10 billion for AFDC payments and child welfare services.

Dependent children are people who are under eighteen and who have no parents or guardian, who need special treatment for their physical or mental health that their parents are unable to provide, or whose parents have asked that custody be given to another because they are *unable* to care for them.  (Minn. Stat. §260.015 (6))

*What happens if someone claims that I am neglected or dependent?*

The procedures in these cases are nearly the same as in delinquent cases. There must be a petition, notice to the parents, and a hearing before the juvenile court.  The rules are a little different, for dependency and neglect only have to be proved by a preponderence of the evidence (the most logical explanation) and not beyond a reasonable doubt, and the juvenile does not have the right to remain silent.  Both the parents and the minor do have a right to a lawyer, and have all of the other important rights that they would have in a delinquency case.  (Minn. J.C.R. 2-1, 2-2, 2-3)

*What can the judge do to me if I am found dependent or neglected?*

The judge can order that:

1.  You be placed under the supervision of the county welfare board or child placement agency in your own home under rules set by the judge.

*Why do some parents abandon their children?*

**2.** Transfer legal custody to the county welfare board or a child placement agency so that they and not your parents are responsible for you.

**3.** If you are in need of special treatment or care for your mental or physical health, your parents or someone else provide it.

None of these orders may be for more than a year, although the judge may review the situation, order an investigation, and renew the order each year until you are twenty-one. (Minn. Stat. §260.191)

## LOSS OF PARENTAL RIGHTS

*What is a termination of the parents' right to custody?*

In certain very serious cases, the juvenile court has the power to end your parents' control over you and their responsibility for you completely. Termination cases are brought by petition and the procedure is very similar to that in delinquency proceedings. A notice and full hearing are required to protect both the parents and the minor. The court may terminate your parents' rights if:

1. They have abandoned you.

2. They have continuously refused to give you necessary care.

3. They have the money to care for you but haven't supported you.

4. Their conduct is harmful to your health or morals.

5. You have previously been found dependent or neglected and your parents have failed to correct the problem. (Minn. Stat. §§260.221 and .231)

*What will the judge do with me if my parents' rights are terminated?*

The judge can transfer guardianship and legal custody to:

1. The Minnesota Commissioner of Public Welfare.

2. A child placement agency.

3. Any other person of good character.

The person receiving custody will have all of the rights that your parents had before their rights were terminated.


## FOSTER FAMILIES

*What is a foster family?*

A family licensed by the state to provide twenty-four-hour care, during a temporary period, for children who are unrelated to the foster family. Although most foster families care for children only until the child can be returned to his or her natural parents, some placements are planned to last until the child reaches eighteen years of age.

*Who can place me in a foster home?*

Your parents, a judge, the county welfare board, or a child placement agency.

*When would I be placed in a foster home?*

Some reasons for placement are that the parents are unable to care for you properly, that you have been declared neglected or dependent, that your parents' rights have been terminated, or that a judge so orders.

## MEDICAL CARE

*Can I get medical care without my parents' consent?*

Although parents' consent is usually required, minors can get certain kinds of medical care in some cases without their parents' consent.

1.  Minors who are living separately from their parents and managing their money, even though their parents still support them, may consent to all kinds of medical and health care.  (Minn. Stat. §144.341)

2.  Any minor who has been married or who has had a child may consent to any kind of medical or other health care.  (Minn. Stat. §144.342)

3.  Any minor may give consent to medical care to determine or treat pregnancy, or to treat venereal disease or problems of drug or alcohol abuse. (Minn. Stat. §144.343)

4.  Emergency medical care may be given to minors if the doctor believes that the minor's health or life would be endangered by delay, and contacting the parents would cause delay.  (Minn. Stat. §144.344)

*If a minor is living at home, her parents must be notified before she has an abortion.*

*If I get medical care under these rules, will the doctor tell my parents?*

A doctor or other medical person may inform the minor's parents of such treatment only if the health of the patient would be seriously jeopardized if they weren't told. (Minn. Stat. §144.346)

*Must my parents give consent for an abortion if I am under eighteen?*

No. In *Bellotti v. Baird*, the U.S. Supreme Court ruled a Massachusetts statute unconstitutional that required minors seeking abortion to obtain either parental consent or judicial approval after they notified their parents.

*Must my parents be notified before I can have an abortion if I am under eighteen?*

Effective August 1, 1981, before an abortion can be performed on an unmarried woman younger than eighteen living at home, a forty-eight-hour notice to her parents must be given. Notice is not required if the abortion is necessary to prevent the woman's death or if she has been the victim of sexual abuse and reported it.

## RUNNING AWAY

*What can happen if I run away from home?*

If you are under eighteen, a police officer may take you into custody immediately, without a warrant, if you have run away from your parents or if the officer reasonably believes that you have. (Minn. Stat. §260.165) No arrest warrant is necessary because this is not an arrest; the police only take you into custody to stop you from running away. (Minn. Stat. §260.165)

*What can the police do with me after they pick me up?*

Your parents will be notified immediately and you will be released to go home with them if they agree to bring you to court in case that is necessary. However, you can be detained for twenty-four hours (excluding Saturdays, Sundays, and holidays) in a detention home, a foster care facility, a Minnesota Corrections Authority reception center, or any other suitable place if your welfare requires it, or if it is necessary for the "protection of the community." The authorities cannot detain you for more than forty-eight hours without the permission of the juvenile court judge. (Minn. Stat. §260.171)



*What if I run away to another state?*

Your parents can still get you back. Minnesota, along with forty-one other states and the District of Columbia, belongs to the Interstate Compact on Juveniles. This means that the governments of all of these states have agreed to return runaway minors to their homes in other states. (Minn. Stat. §260.51)

*How does this work?*

The procedure is complicated, but usually it begins when your parents ask a court in the state of Minnesota to send a *requisition* (request) to the other state for your return. They must show the court that you are not an emancipated minor and that by running away you have endangered your own welfare or that of others. When the courts or governor of the other state get the requisition, the police there may take you into custody. The courts of that state will then decide whether or not the requisition is legal and, if it is, return you to Minnesota. (Minn. Stat. §260.51)


## EMANCIPATION

*What is emancipation?*

**Emancipation** refers to the ending of the legal ties between parents and child. Minnesota law does not provide any exact definition. In general the parents give up their right to the child's services and their right to control the child. Also, the parents no longer have to support the child. (*Taubert v. Taubert*, 103 Minn. 247, 114 N.W. 763 (1908))

Emancipation does not have to be complete; it can be partial or limited. For example, the parents' right to services and control may end, but they still may have the duty to support the child. On the other hand, there may be complete emancipation even though the child still lives with his or her parents. (*Taubert v. Taubert*, 103 Minn. 247, 114 N.W. 763 (1908))

*When does emancipation occur?*

It is difficult to tell when emancipation occurs. You are automatically emancipated when you become eighteen, although it can happen earlier. You are also emancipated when you marry. Parents and child don't have to have a written or oral agreement for emancipation to occur. Normally, you can tell if a minor is emancipated by looking at his or her conduct and that of the parents. (*In re Settlement of Horton*, 212 Minn. 7, 2 N.W.2d 749 (1942))

*Do my parents ever have to support me after I'm emancipated?*

Yes. If you are ever so poor that you would have to go on welfare, your parents and other close relatives could be required to support you regardless of your age or the fact that you had been emancipated. (Minn. Stat.§§ 261.01 and 256.457)


## PATERNITY AND ADOPTION

*What is a paternity suit?*

A paternity suit is a lawsuit to decide whether a particular man is the father of an illegitimate child and to require him to support that child if he is the father.

emancipation: to release a child from the control of his or her parents.

**WHAT
DO
YOU
THINK?**

Jamie Juarez, an eighteen-year-old senior in high school, discovers accidentally that he is an adopted child. His adoptive mother refuses to discuss the matter. Should Jamie have a right to know who his natural parents are? What are the pros and cons of permitting Jamie to do this from his perspective? His adoptive parents' perspective? His natural parents' perspective? Should adopted children be told they are adopted?

The father of an illegitimate child is liable for the expenses of the mother's pregnancy, her medical bills, and support for her during the eight weeks before and the eight weeks after the child is born. He must also pay for the support and education of the child until it is an adult. (Minn. Stat. §257.251)

*Can a minor be sued for paternity?*

Yes.

*Can a girl's parents start a paternity suit?*

No, unless they have provided some of the support for the girl and the baby that they want to recover from the father. Normally only the mother, the child, the public welfare authorities, or the county attorney can start a paternity suit. (Minn. Stat. §§257.252 and 257.254)

*If a minor girl has an illegitimate child, can she give it up for adoption without her parents' consent?*

If the girl is under eighteen she must have the consent of her parents to give the child up for **adoption**. (Minn. Stat. §259.24 (2))

**adoption:** a device for establishing a legal relationship of parent and child not already so related by law.

*Does an unmarried father have anything to say about whether or not the child is given up for adoption?*

This area of the law is very uncertain right now. Minnesota law says that the consent of the father of an illegitimate child is required if the father's name appears on the birth certificate; if the father has substantially supported the child; if the father and mother married within 325 days before the child's birth or within 10 days after the child's birth; if the father has been judged the parent by a court of law; or if the father within 90 days of the child's birth or within 60 days of the child's placement for adoption gives an affidavit to the Minnesota Department of Health, Division of Vital Statistics, stating his intention to retain parental rights. (Minn. Stat. §259.24) Notice of a hearing for adoption of an illegitimate child must be given to the parents. (Minn. Stat. §259.26) The father may try to convince the judge that he should have custody. The United States Supreme Court has also said that the father of an illegitimate child must be given notice of an adoption proceeding, and a hearing to consider his fitness as a father must be held prior to adoption. (*Stanley v. Illinois,* 405 U.S. 645 (1972))

## PROBLEM 1

Tom, age seventeen, and Teresa, age sixteen, have been dating for two years. Teresa discovers she is pregnant and decides to have the baby but to give it up for adoption. She does not want to get married and have a family at age sixteen but wants to go to college so she can be an architect. Tom wants to marry her, but if she won't marry him, he would like custody of the baby.

Tom's parents have said they will help him take care of the baby.  Teresa
does not want Tom to have the baby.

1. What advice would you give Tom?

2. Can he get custody of the baby?

3. What advice would you give Teresa?

4. Can she keep Tom from getting custody?

# 4

# DISSOLUTION OF MARRIAGE

**CONTENTS**



Dissolution of marriage used to be called divorce. The divorce laws were based on fault and one party could get a divorce only if it could be shown that the other party was at fault in some way. States have been adopting no-fault statutes on the theory that if the marriage is irretrievably broken, two people should not be forced to stay together even if no one can be clearly shown to be at fault. In an attempt to eliminate hostility between the parties, even the name of the action has been changed from divorce to dissolution.

This chapter is designed to tell you when two people can dissolve their marriage, and explore some of the consequences arising from such an action.

## CASE STUDY

*Sam and Susan, both eighteen, get married during their senior year of high school. They graduate and both go to college. During their second year of college, Sam decides the marriage was a mistake and wants to be free of Susan, who does not want to dissolve the marriage.*

1. What can Susan do to prevent the dissolution of the marriage?

2. What are the grounds Sam must allege?

---

**SELF-QUIZ**

---

Before you read the chapter, try the following quiz. Answer each question as best you can, based on your general knowledge. When you have read the chapter, go back to see whether or not you have changed your mind about any of the answers.

**1.** A marriage cannot be dissolved if one of the spouses thinks the marriage is not irretrievably broken. _______ True _______ False

**2.** A child has no input into which parent gets custody. _______ True _______ False

**3.** Fathers cannot get custody of preschool-age children. _______ True _______ False

**4.** A name changed upon marriage can be changed again upon dissolution of that marriage. _______ True _______ False

**5.** Alimony is money that is paid by the husband to the wife after their marriage is dissolved. _______ True _______ False

**6.** Upon dissolution, marital property is divided fifty-fifty between husband and wife. _______ True _______ False

**7.** Custody is always given to the mother or father. _______ True _______ False

**8.** The parents of the mother or father who did not gain custody have no right to visit their grandchildren. _______ True _______ False

## ANNULMENT

*What is the difference between annulment and dissolution?*

**annulment:** a proceeding that declares a marriage null and void at the time of its beginning.

**dissolution:** a proceeding that declares a marriage void from the date of the dissolution.

An **annulment** is a proceeding brought in limited circumstances to declare a marriage null and void at the time of its beginning. A **dissolution** proceeding declares a marriage void from the date of the dissolution decree but leaves the marriage valid up to that time. Grounds for annulment include one or both of the parties being underage, and lack of capacity to consent to marriage because of the influence of alcohol, drugs, or other incapacitating substances. (Minn. Stat. §§518.01, 518.03)  If the parties voluntarily live together as husband and wife after attaining the legal age for marriage, an annulment cannot be granted. (Minn. Stat. §518.04)

*What is the effect of an annulment on the parties' rights and responsibilities?*

The statutory provisions applicable to dissolution proceedings  (Minn. Stat. §§518.54 to 518.66) are also applicable to annulment proceedings and determine property rights of the spouses, maintenance, and support and custody of the children. (Minn. Stat. §518.03)  Any children born of a marriage later annulled are deemed legitimate. (Minn. Stat. §517.19)

# GROUNDS

*What are the grounds for getting a dissolution of a marriage?*

A dissolution of a marriage will be granted when the court finds that there has been an irretrievable breakdown of the marriage relationship. (See Minn. Stat. §518.06)

*Will a dissolution of marriage be granted if one of the parties denies that there has been an irretrievable breakdown of the marriage relationship?*

Yes. If one of the parties says the marriage is broken and one says it is not, their disagreement is evidence of marital discord. The statute states that in this situation, the marriage will be dissolved only upon a finding by the court that there is not reasonable prospect of reconciliation. This finding must be supported by evidence that the parties have lived separate and apart not less than 180 days before filing the petition, or that there is serious marital discord adversely affecting the attitude of one or both of the parties toward the marriage.

# NAME

*If I changed my name upon marriage, can I change it again upon dissolution of my marriage?*

Yes. The court in a dissolution proceeding shall change the name of either party who had acquired the name of his or her spouse back to that person's family name upon request. (Minn. Stat. §518.27)

# CHILD CUSTODY

*If my parents are getting a dissolution, who represents me?*

In all actions for dissolution in which custody or visitation of a minor child is an issue, the court may appoint a guardian ad litem to represent the interests of any such child. (Minn. Stat. §518.165)

*How does the court decide who gets custody of the child?*

In deciding custody matters, the court considers the best interests of the child. This means that the court looks at all relevant factors including the wishes of the parents; the wishes of the child; the interaction and interrelationship of the child and the parents, siblings, and other persons who may significantly affect the child's best interests; the child's adjustment to home, school, and community; and the mental and physical health of all individuals involved. (Minn. Stat. §518.17)

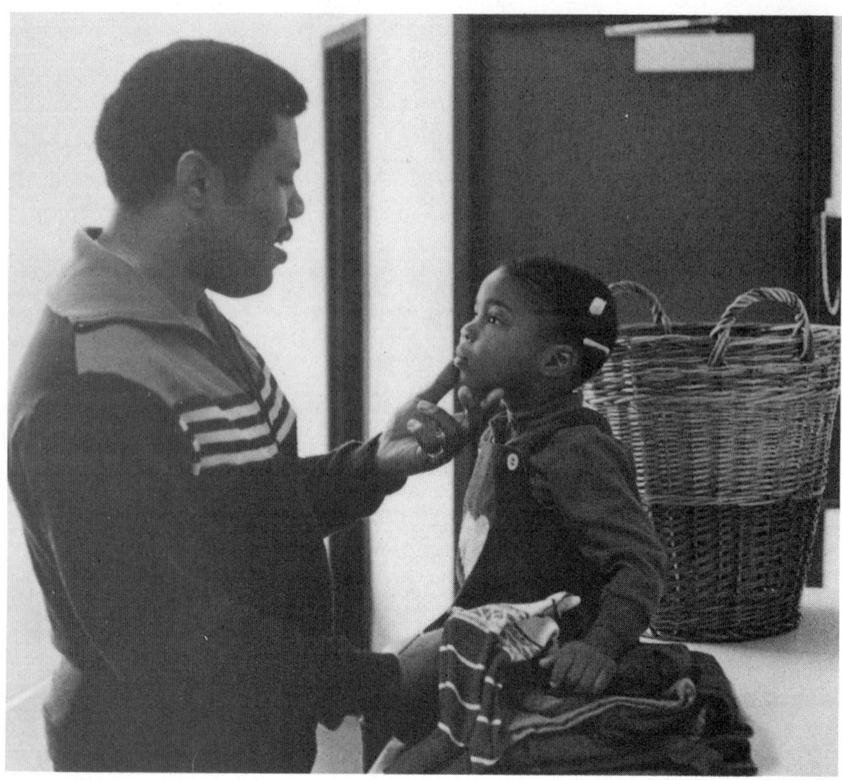

*Custody depends on the best interests of the child.*



*Do children have any say about where they want to live?*

The court may interview the child in the judge's chambers to ascertain the child's wishes as to the custodian.  (Minn. Stat. §518.166)

*Does the court automatically give girls and little children to the mother and boys to the father?*

No.  It is against the law for the court to prefer one parent over the other solely on the basis of the sex of the parents when determining the parent with whom a child shall remain.  The court must consider the best interests of the child, as explained earlier.  (Minn. Stat. §518.17)

*Will the court split up brothers and sisters in a custody case?*

The court is interested in what is in the best interest for each child.  The court takes into account the interaction and interrelationship of each child with the brothers and sisters in deciding what is in the child's best interests.  If the court believes it is in the best interests of each of the children that they not be split up, this will be decreed.  (Minn. Stat. §518.17)

*Can I live with my older sister (or brother) instead of my mom or my dad?*

Again, the court is interested in what is in your best interests, and if this arrangement is considered in your best interests, it will be decreed. (Minn. Stat. §518.17)

*What happens if I want to live with my mom now and later on I decide I would rather live with my dad? Do I have to stay with the person to whom custody was originally granted?*

The court has power to change a custody decree if it finds that a change has occurred in the circumstances of the child or the custodian, and that modification is necessary to serve the best interests of the child. In applying these standards, the court will not change the custody arrangement unless the custodian agrees to the modification, the child has been integrated into the family of the proposed custodian with the consent of the present custodian, or the child's present environment is significantly harmful to the child and the harm likely to be caused by a change in environment is outweighed by the advantage of a change to the child. (Minn. Stat. §518.18)

## VISITATION

*Does the noncustodial parent get to visit the child?*

Yes. The court will grant such rights of visitation as to enable the noncustodial parent to maintain a relationship with the child that will be in the best interests of the child. (Minn. Stat. §518.175)

*If the noncustodial parent doesn't pay support as ordered by the court, can the custodial parent deny visitation?*

Failure to pay because of inability to pay shall not be sufficient cause for denial of visitation. (Minn. Stat. §518.175)

*Does the court ever restrict visitation rights?*

Yes, if the court finds that visitation is likely to endanger the child's physical or emotional health, or impair his or her emotional development.

*Do grandparents have any visitation rights?*

When the parents' marriage is dissolved, a court may, upon request of a grandparent, grant reasonable visitation rights to the child. (Minn. Stat. §257.022)

*Visitation rights may include grandparents.*

## CHILD SUPPORT

*Does the father have to support the children after dissolution of a marriage?*

**child support:** the legal obligation of parents to contribute to the economic maintenance, including education, of their children.

By statute the court may order either or both parents to pay **child support** after considering all relevant factors including financial resources and needs of the child, financial resources and needs of custodial parent and noncustodial parent, the standard of living the child would have enjoyed had the marriage not been dissolved, and the physical and emotional condition of the child and his or her educational needs.  (Minn. Stat. §518.17)

**TABLE 4-1   Spousal and Child Support**

| Net Monthly Income | Spouse Alone | One Child Alone (More than one, not over amount in Column 6) | Spouse and One Child | Spouse and Two Children | Spouse and Three or More Children |
|---|---|---|---|---|---|
| $ 400 | $100 | $ 80 | $100 | $100 | $ 100 |
| 500 | 150 | 75-100 | 150 | 150 | 150 |
| 600 | 200 | 125-150 | 250 | 250 | 250 |
| 700 | 250 | 150-175 | 350 | 350 | 350 |
| 800 | 250 | 175-225 | 375 | 400 | 400 |
| 900 | 300 | 175-225 | 400 | 425 | 450 |
| 1000 | 325 | 200-250 | 450 | 475 | 500 |
| 1200 | 400 | 225-275 | 500 | 550 | 600 |
| 1500 | 450 | 250-300 | 600 | 675 | 750 |
| 1750 | 525 | 275-325 | 700 | 800 | 875 |
| 2000 | 600 | 300-350 | 800 | 900 | 1000 |
| Above 2000 | 33 1/3% | | 40% | 45% | 50% |

*Which column represents maintenance?  Child support?  Do you think these amounts are fair? Should wives be required to pay alimony to husbands?*

## SPOUSAL MAINTENANCE

*Does the husband have to pay alimony to the wife?*

By statute either party may be required to pay what is now called maintenance rather than **alimony**.  The court considers the need of the party requesting maintenance and the ability of the other spouse to pay. The court also considers age, physical and emotional condition of the spouse seeking maintenance, the duration of marriage, and the time necessary for the party seeking maintenance to find appropriate employment.  When maintenance is granted, it is usually the husband who is required to pay for the support and maintenance of the wife.  However, maintenance is often ordered for a limited period of time during which the supported spouse is expected to get a job.  (Minn. Stat. §518.552)

**alimony:** court-ordered payments by a divorced spouse to the other spouse for ongoing personal support.

## PROPERTY SETTLEMENT

*How is property of the marriage divided?*

Minnesota courts are given broad authority to make a just and equitable division of the marital property of the parties without considering any marital misconduct. (Minn. Stat. §518.58) The division of the property of the marriage is particularly important because neither spouse can do anything with the property until ownership is determined.  For instance, while the parties are married, neither can sell or give away any real estate

*The court may order child support depending on the financial resources and needs of both the parents and children.*

without the written consent of the other. This stems from the right of a spouse to certain property at the death of the other spouse. No buyer would pay for land if he or she realized that on the death of the spouse selling the land, the other spouse could then assert a right of ownership. For this reason any deed requires identification of the seller as to marital status, and if the seller is married, the signature of the other spouse is required before the property can be totally transferred.

## PROBLEM 1

Scott and Mary work in the same department store. Mary was a sixteen-year-old part-time clerk still attending high school. Scott was a twenty-year-old sporting goods clerk. They decided to get married but Mary's parents would not consent. A friend at the store told them mistakenly that in a neighboring state a girl can get married without consent at the age of seventeen. The neighboring state actually has the same laws as Minnesota.

Scott and Mary traveled to the neighboring state and were married. Wanting to be safe about Mary's age, they decided at the last minute to tell the clerk that Mary was eighteen.

For a while the marriage went smoothly. Mary's parents finally accepted Scott as a son-in-law and helped them make a down payment on a house. Scott and Mary had a child, forcing Mary to stop working. After three years, Scott started drinking heavily and stayed away from home for days at a time. Mary learned that during these times Scott was staying with women he met while drinking.

Mary has told Scott that she wants to terminate the marriage and that she is going to sell some property she inherited from her grandmother last year to obtain independent funds. Scott consults an attorney and says he will block the sale by refusing to consent to it, just to get even with her.

**1.** Can Mary have the marriage annulled as invalid, or must she go through the process of dissolution? Should Mary be thinking about dissolving the marriage at this stage of their relationship?

**2.** If she must petition the court for dissolution, on what grounds could she base her petition?

**3.** What are some of the problems that may be encountered in the dissolution process?

**4.** Can Scott block Mary's sale of her inherited property?

**5.** Assume the dissolution petition is approved and Scott refuses to help support his family. Besides the legal steps that can be taken against him, do Mary's parents have any further obligations to her?


## PROBLEM 2

Mabel Milkweed, born Feruary 23, 1945, and James Crabgrass, born March 20, 1944, were married May 28, 1964, in Grinnell, Iowa. The couple, being very forward-looking in their thinking, decided to use the combined name of Milkweed-Crabgrass after their marriage.

Mabel and James adopted a Vietnamese boy, Park Reed, in 1970. Park was born August 5, 1969. On May 1, 1974, a daughter, Mary Louise, was born. These two children attend a Catholic school, kindergarten through eighth grade, which costs $350 per child for the 1979-80 school year. Park is going to need extensive orthodontic work beginning in seventh grade.

Mabel has earned her Masters of Science and is currently working as a nursing administrator at a take-home salary of $1,200 per month. Mabel's fringe benefits include a $20,000 life insurance policy and the availability of Group Health coverage, which she didn't elect to use because the family chose to use James's Blue Cross-Blue Shield coverage. James is an engineer with 3M and has worked there since July 1, 1966. His take-home salary is $1,400 per month. Among the fringe benefits received by James are health and dental insurance for the family, all paid by 3M, a $50,000 life insurance group policy, and participation in a noncontributory pension absolutely vested. If James's employment were terminated today, under this pension plan he would receive $154 per month for life, beginning at age 65. The longer he stays at 3M, the larger the pension would be.

Mabel and James have decided they want a divorce, but they are still living in the same house, at 1406 Edmund Boulevard, St. Paul, Minnesota 55104. They both want custody of the children so neither is willing to vacate the house. They had a guest bedroom into which James has moved.

Their assets are as follows:

- 1976 Chevrolet Chevette

- 1980 Pontiac Phoenix

- 1968 Ford Mustang Convertible

- Household goods and furnishings (includes silver place setting for twelve)

- Savings Account—$1,000

- Homestead—1979 estimated market value is $75,000. Current mortgage balance is $26,000. (They also put a new roof on last summer and have 1½ years of payments to make on a home improvement loan at the rate of $135 per month, with the last payment due August 5, 1981).

- Lake Frontage—Purchased on contract for deed for $20,000. Monthly payments are $100. They are selling this land on contract for deed, receiving payments of $130 per month. Mabel and James will have paid for the land in June, 1990. Their purchasers will make the last payment in June, 1995.

- $5,000 of stock inherited from Mabel's mother

Their liabilities are as follows:

- Mortgage—$25,000

- Home Improvement Loan—$2,400

- Contract for Deed—$18,000

- Dayton's, Powers, Visa, and Montgomery Ward—$2,000

- Checking reserve at local bank—$1,000

You will be working in teams of two, one attorney representing Mabel and one attorney representing James. You are to reach a settlement agreement (stipulation) on all of Mabel and James's disputes, which will be presented to the court as the basis for a default judgment and decree. Among the issues that must be decided are custody of the children, child support, spousal support, payment of debts, and distribution of property. Write a detailed settlement agreement resolving all issues between the parties.

# 5

# CRIMINAL AND JUVENILE JUSTICE

## CONTENTS



As we learned in Chapter 1 on civil law, criminal laws have a dual purpose. They seek to regulate the conduct of an individual within society by defining certain kinds of behavior that society will not tolerate. The expression of the limits of approved behavior protects the interests of the vast majority of citizens who are law-abiding. Criminal laws also provide a punishment if the individual's conduct falls within one of these prohibited types of behavior. If you violate a criminal law, you may be arrested, tried, convicted, and punished by the state.

The definition of prohibited behavior has been assigned in our society to legislative bodies at the federal, state, and local levels. For example, in Minnesota an act is not a crime unless a legislative body has said it is. These bodies also provide general guidelines as to the punishment for each offense. The enforcement of these laws is left to the police, the court systems, and the correctional authorities.

This chapter will give you some idea of what is a crime and the various things that can or do occur when a person is arrested for committing a crime. Particular emphasis has been placed on the rights of the individual in the system. You will note that here, as in civil law, a young person may be treated the same as anybody else, or given certain additional safeguards, depending on the circumstances. The first section also contains some explanation of crimes or unlawful acts young people most frequently become involved in and a chart of adult criminal laws in Minnesota.

## CASE STUDY

*Roger, a thirteen-year-old with a record as a troublemaker, is greeted at the front door of his family's home by two uniformed police officers who claim he stole a car that was found smashed into a school's loading dock. The car's owner claims the television set in the back seat was removed.*

1. Before Roger says anything, what should he know about his rights?

2. Can the officers question him?

3. What might be some possible steps in Roger's case?

---

**SELF-QUIZ**

---

Before you read the chapter, try the following quiz. Answer the questions as best you can, based on your general knowledge. When you have read the chapter, go back to see whether or not you have changed your mind about any of the answers.

1. A crime is any act for which you can be arrested or given a ticket. _______ True _______ False

2. A fourteen-year-old may be tried for murder in Minnesota and sentenced to prison. _______ True _______ False

3. In deciding whether or not a sixteen-year-old should be tried as a juvenile or as an adult, a judge considers only the young person's maturity and past record. _______ True _______ False

4. If a young person under eighteen is tried as an adult, he or she must be put in prison like an adult. _______ True _______ False

5. A young person accused of a crime has a strict right to a lawyer, and unless he or she has an opportunity to have legal counsel, no testimony given by him or her can be used as discriminating evidence. _______ True _______ False

6. When someone starts a fight with you, you have the right to defend yourself by any means available. _______ True _______ False

7. Painting your class numerals on the town water tower, a railroad bridge, or the walls of the school can be a felony. _______ True _______ False

8. Helping a friend hide from the police can subject you to the same degree of criminal responsibility as your friend. _______ True _______ False

9. Your father gives you two eight-dollar tickets to a Vikings game. You find later that you cannot go. It is not illegal for you to sell them to a friend for twenty dollars. _______ True _______ False

10. In an exchange of shots during an armed robbery, one of the robbers misses and kills his partner. He can be convicted of murder. _______ True _______ False

11. The term *juvenile court* refers to a special set of rules that judges must use when young persons are accused of crime or have family problems. _______ True _______ False

**12.** The minimum age for a person to appear in juvenile court is sixteen. _______ True _______ False

**13.** Young persons may go to juvenile court if they need a judge's permission to get married or if they are abandoned by their parents. _______ True _______ False

**14.** One of the rights afforded young people in the juvenile court is the right to refuse to be tried as a juvenile. _______ True _______ False

**15.** If all evidence at the delinquency hearing in the juvenile court points to that young people being a delinquent, the judge must remove the young person from the parents' custody. _______ True _______ False

**16.** You cannot appeal a finding of delinquency by the juvenile court. _______ True _______ False

**17.** The juvenile court may terminate the rights of parents if they refuse to provide necessary care and support. _______ True _______ False

**18.** A juvenile court judge may recommend suspension or cancellation of your license for serious traffic offenses. _______ True _______ False

**19.** A young person claims not to be delinquent. Therefore, the court cannot order a physical or mental examination unless the young person agrees. _______ True _______ False

**20.** The sole function of the probation officer is to spy on people placed on probation. _______ True _______ False

**21.** Probation officers can take a person into custody on their own if that person violates the terms of probation. _______ True _______ False

**22.** All taking of human life is a crime. _______ True _______ False

**23.** If I am accused of a serious crime I am tried by a grand jury, for a less serious crime by a petit jury. _______ True _______ False

**24.** All lying is a crime. _______ True _______ False

**25.** I have a right to refuse to answer questions regarding a crime. _______ True _______ False

**26.** I cannot be forced to testify in court on a matter that does not concern me. _______ True _______ False

**27.** I cannot be punished before a court for conduct that is not criminal. _______ True _______ False

**28.** My buddy is hiding from the police. I tell the police he or she has gone out of town. I am guilty of a crime. _______ True _______ False

**29.** If I am charged with being the father of an illegitimate child in a paternity proceeding, I may refuse to answer questions concerning my association with the child's mother on the grounds that it may incriminate me. _______ True _______ False

**30.** I hear about some incident in the life of one of my teachers that, if widely known, would result in ridicule or disgrace. I threaten to broadcast this information unless I get a good grade. I am guilty of a crime. _______ True _______ False

**31.** I am angry at a certain person so I go to the police and accuse this person of a crime. I know no crime can be proved but I want to put my enemy to the trouble of a hearing to be cleared. I can be punished. _______ True _______ False

**32.** I see a "No Smoking" sign near a tank containing flammable material, but I light a cigarette. I can be punished. _______ True _______ False

**33.** A merchant without a warrant can arrest me for shoplifting. _______ True _______ False

*What is a crime?*

Minnesota law defines a *crime* as conduct that is forbidden by a statute and for which the person may be sentenced to prison. (Minn. Stat. §609.02) There are three different types of crimes:

1. *Felonies*—crimes punishable by more than one year in prison. (Minn. Stat. §609.02)

2. *Misdemeanors*—crimes punishable by a jail sentence of not more than ninety days, or a fine of not more than $500, or both. (Minn. Stat. §609.02)

3. *Gross Misdemeanors*—all other crimes—that is, crimes punishable by a sentence of ninety-one days to one year, or a fine of more than $500, or both. (Minn. Stat. §609.02)

*Is it a crime to park in a no parking zone?*

No. This and other minor violations are petty misdemeanors. They are punishable by a fine not to exceed $100, not a jail sentence. (Minn. Stat. §609.02)

## SPECIFIC OFFENSES

FIRST DEGREE
  MURDER
Premeditation
Intent
Causes death of a person

SECOND DEGREE
  MURDER
Intent
Causes death of a person

*I see another person being attacked by a man with a knife and I cannot stop the attacker, so I take the attacker's knife and stab him, and he dies from the resulting wound. Am I guilty of murder?*

You might be charged with it, but in your defense if you could prove you were acting to prevent this person from killing or gravely injuring someone else, your act might be justifiable. Intentional taking of a life is not legal except in specific instances, one of which is to prevent injury to yourself or another. (Minn. Stat. §609.065) Intent is a factor in determining the crime you have committed. (Minn. Stat. §609.185)

*Can I get into trouble for fighting?*

Yes. It is an assault to injure or try to injure another person, or purposely make people fear they will be hurt by you. (Minn. Stat. §609.22) If you use a knife or other dangerous weapon in a fight, you may be guilty of the felony of aggravated assault, a very serious crime. (Minn. Stat. §609.225) If you fight in a public place where it bothers or disturbs other people, you could be convicted of disorderly conduct, a misdemeanor. (Minn. Stat. §609.72)

*What is the penalty for bombing?*

If you intentionally bomb a building used as a dwelling, whether the inhabitant is present or not; or bomb a building connected with a dwelling; or a building not used as a dwelling, if the presence of a person in the

*Fighting with the intent of injuring another person is an assault.*

building is a reasonable possibility; you may be guilty of aggravated arson, which is punishable by imprisonment for not more than twenty years, or a fine of $20,000, or both. If you destroy a building that is not inhabited, you are guilty of arson in the second degree, which has a penalty of up to ten years in prison, or a fine of $10,000, or both. If the property damaged or destroyed is personal property, for example a car, and is worth more than $100, the destruction by explosives or fire is arson in the third degree and is subject to imprisonment for not more than five years, or a fine of $5,000, or both. (Minn. Stat. §§609.561, 609.562, 609.563)

*Can I get in trouble for hiding a friend from the police?*

Yes.  If your friend has committed a felony and you hide him or her from the police, you have committed a felony too and could be imprisoned for three years, or fined $3,000, or both.  If your friend has committed a misdemeanor, you would be guilty of a misdemeanor too.  (Minn. Stat. §609.495)  This section does not apply if the person at the time of hiding is related to the offender as husband, wife, parent, or child.  (Minn. Stat. §609.495(2))

*Is it illegal for me to have intercourse with my girl friend?*

It is illegal for a person to have intercourse with a single woman.  (Minn. Stat. §609.34)  This is a misdemeanor.  Also, if a person is under thirteen and you are thirty-six months older, intercourse can be sexual conduct in the first degree subject to imprisonment for twenty years.  If he or she is between the ages of thirteen and sixteen, and you are four years older and have some authority over the younger person, this is also sexual conduct in the first degree.  If he or she is between the ages of thirteen and sixteen and you are three years older, this might be sexual conduct in the second degree, punishable by imprisonment of up to fifteen years.

*Is it illegal to go away with my girl friend even if we are going to get married?*

Yes.  If she is under eighteen and you take her away to get married without her parents' consent, you are guilty of abduction, a gross misdemeanor.  (Minn. Stat. §609.265)

*If my girl friend gets pregnant can I be arrested?*

No, not for the pregnancy.  However, it is a misdemeanor to have intercourse with someone who is not your spouse.  You might have to pay for her expenses, and the expenses of the child (see Chapter 3 on paternity).  It is a crime, punishable by imprisonment for two years, or a fine of $2,000, or both, to leave the state if you know that your girl friend is pregnant and leave in order to avoid having to pay.  (Minn. Stat. §609.31)  It is also a crime, punishable by imprisonment for up to five years, to fail to support a child, if the failure continues for more than ninety days and there is no legal excuse for that failure.  (Minn. Stat. §609.375)



*What is the penalty for joyriding in a car?*

If you simply take somebody's car for a drive without his consent, you are guilty of unauthorized use of a motor vehicle, which is punishable by imprisonment for three years, or a fine of $3,000, or both.  (Minn. Stat. §609.55) If you take somebody else's car and intend to keep it or sell it instead of returning it after a ride, you are guilty of theft and could be imprisoned for up to five to ten years, depending on the value of the automobile.  (Minn. Stat. §609.52)

*Is it illegal to buy something that I think is stolen?*

Yes, it is theft to receive or buy stolen property intentionally.  (Minn. Stat. §609.53)

*If I find money or something else valuable, do I have to try to find the owner?*

Yes.  It is theft to keep lost property without making a reasonable effort to find the real owner and return the property.  (Minn. Stat. §609.52)

*What can happen if I use somebody else's credit card without permission?*

You would be guilty of misusing a credit card, which is a misdemeanor. (Minn. Stat. §609.545)  You could also be found guilty of theft.  (Minn. Stat. §609.52)

*Does theft include shoplifting?*

Yes.  (Minn. Stat. §609.52)

*Is it illegal to sew an American flag on my clothes?*

Probably not, although the Minnesota Supreme Court has never had a case like this.  It is a misdemeanor to mutilate, defile, or cast contempt on the flag publicly, or to display a flag if you have put any word, mark, or design on it. (Minn. Stat. §609.40)  This probably applies only to conduct that is actually disrespectful.  It is not clear whether it applies to flying a flag upside down for a protest.

An interesting case concerning a similar statute was heard by the United States Supreme Court.  The case is entitled *Street v. State of New York*, 394 U.S. 576 (1969).  In this case Mr. Street, upset at the killing of James Meredith, a civil rights leader, burned his flag in New York City.  The Supreme Court stated that his conduct was a form of speech and was protected by the Fourteenth Amendment of the United States Constitution.

*If I call somebody in the middle of the night and hang up, can I get in trouble even though it is only a joke?*

Yes.  It is a misdemeanor to call another person and hang up without giving your name if you intend to harass or annoy another person.  (Minn. Stat. §609.79)

---

**WHAT DO YOU THINK?**

David decided to steal a radio from a SuperAmerica store. As he is leaving an attendant chases David.  David told his friend that if anyone tried to stop him he would kill that person.  David does kill the attendant.  What crime has David committed?  Why?

---

**LITTLE KNOWN LAWS OF MINNESOTA**

1.  In Minnesota, women are forbidden from showing up on the street dressed as Santa Claus.
2.  An old law in Brainerd, Minnesota, ordered that every male must grow a beard.

*(continued on next page)*

3. Women may not shine their shoes on Saturday in Marshall, Minnesota.

4. In Minneapolis, it is against the law to install a bathtub in your home unless it has legs.

5. In St. Paul, you may not take pigs into any public building.

6. A child under twelve may only use a telephone when accompanied by a parent in Blue Earth, Minnesota.

7. The legal punishment in Minneapolis for double-parking is to be put on a chain gang and fed only bread and water.

8. An old Minnesota law required that men's and women's underwear may not be hung on the same clothesline at the same time.

9. In Pine Island, Minnesota, a man must tip his hat to every passing cow.

Adapted from "You Can't Eat Peanuts in Church" by Barbara Seuling. Adaptation by Karen Rogers, Project Omnibus.

*What other crimes should I know about?*

It is a misdemeanor to:

1. Make a false report of crime to the police. (Minn. Stat. §609.505)

2. Interfere with fire fighters who are trying to put out a fire. (Minn. Stat. §609.60)

3. Remove the serial number or identification number from any property if you do so to keep people from being able to identify it. (Minn. Stat. §609.655)

4. Litter, whether on public or private land. (Minn. Stat. §609.68)

5. Refuse to leave someone's land when you are told to do so. (Minn. Stat. §609.605)

6. Scalp tickets (sell them for a higher price than the price charged for admission by the people putting on the event). (Minn. Stat. §609.805)

7. Intercept a written message that is sealed, knowing you do not have the consent of either the sender or recipient. (Minn. Stat. §609.795)

8. Refuse to surrender a telephone line immediately when informed the line is needed to make an emergency call for medical service or an ambulance, or for assistance from a fire or police agency; or falsely state such a line is needed for an emergency. (Minn. Stat. §609.78)

9. Sell a chance to participate in a lottery. (Minn. Stat. §609.755)

**TABLE 5-1  Common Felonies and Their Penalties**

| OFFENSE | STATUTE SECTION | PENALTY (MAXIMUM) |
| --- | --- | --- |
| Murder | | |
| First Degree<br>(Preplanned or committed during a rape or during burglary, aggravated robbery, kidnapping, or first or second degree assault, or escape from custody, or in tampering with witness, or murder of peace officer or guard) | 609.185 | Life Imprisonment |
| Second Degree<br>(Intentional but not premeditated and unintentional killing during felony, except rape) | 609.19 | 40 Years |
| Third Degree<br>(Nonintentional killing during a felony or while doing something very dangerous) | 609.195 | 25 Years |
| Criminal Sexual Conduct | | |
| First Degree<br>(Sexual relations with a younger person, or under threat, or accomplished with force, or upon a mentally incapacitated or physically helpless person) | 609.342 | 20 Years |
| Manslaughter | | |
| First Degree<br>(Intentional killing in heat of passion or nonintentional killing while committing a violent crime) | 609.20 | 15 Years/$15,000 |
| Second Degree<br>(Nonintentional killing as a result of a very careless act) | 609.205 | 7  Years/$7,000 |
| Criminal Negligence<br>(Negligent killing with a car, plane, or boat) | 609.21 | 5  Years/$5,000 |
| Aggravated Assault<br>(Causing great bodily harm to another) | 609.225 | 10 Years/$10,000 |
| Assault with a weapon | 609.225 | 5  Years/$5,000 |
| Simple Robbery<br>(Taking property of another by force) | 609.24 | 10 Years/$10,000 |
| Aggravated Robbery<br>(Robbery while armed or if great bodily harm is inflicted on the victim) | 609.245 | 20 Years/$20,000 |

**TABLE 5-1——***Continued*

| | | |
|---|---|---|
| Kidnapping<br>(If victim is released<br>without great bodily harm) | 609.25 | 20 Years/$20,000 |
| Otherwise | 609.25 | 40 Years/$40,000 |
| Aggravated Sodomy<br>(Forcing another to engage<br>in sexual relations) | 609.293 | 30 Years |
| Bribery<br>(Giving or accepting bribes<br>involving a public official<br>or a witness) | 609.42 | 10 Years/$10,000 |
| Perjury<br>(Lying under oath) | 609.48 | 5 Years/$5,000 |
| Theft | | |
| (If property is worth<br>more than $2,500) | 609.52 | 10 Years/$10,000 |
| (If $100-$2,500) | 609.52 | 5 Years/$5,000 |
| (If explosives stolen) | 609.52 | 10 Years/$10,000 |
| Arson, First Degree<br>(Danger to others) | 609.561 | 20 Years/$20,000 |
| Arson, Second Degree<br>(Destruction of building) | 609.562 | 10 Years/$10,000 |
| Arson, Third Degree<br>(Personal property worth<br>$100 or more) | 609.563 | 5 Years/$5,000 |
| (Personal property worth<br>less than $100) | 609.563 | 90 Days/$300 |
| Burglary<br>(Breaking and entering to<br>commit a crime) | 609.58 | 20 Years/$20,000 |
| (If done in a dwelling, or<br>burglar possesses a weapon or<br>tool, or burglar commits an<br>assault in an occupied dwelling) | 609.52 | 10 Years/$10,000 |
| (If intent to steal or<br>commit a felony) | 609.52 | 5 Years/$5,000 |
| Forgery | | |
| Aggravated | 609.625 | 10 Years/$10,000 |
| Simple | 609.63 | 3 Years/$3,000 |
| Making False Tax Statement | 609.41 | 1 Years/$1,000 |
| Nonsupport, wife or child | 609.375 | 90 Days/$300 |
| Nonsupport, continued for<br>more than 90 days, no<br>lawful excuse | 609.375 | 5 Years |

## THE JUVENILE COURT

Before considering specific problems of criminal or juvenile justice, we should remember that the United States Constitution establishes certain rights:  the right to be secure in one's person, house, papers, and effects against unreasonable searches and seizures (Fourth Amendment);  not to be held for a "capital" or infamous crime (punishable by death, or life imprisonment where states do not have capital punishment) except on presentment or indictment of a grand jury (Fifth Amendment);  not to be placed in "jeopardy" twice for the same offense (Fifth Amendment);  not to be compelled to testify against oneself (Fifth Amendment);  to be tried on a criminal charge before a jury (Sixth Amendment);  to be told what one is accused of (Sixth Amendment);  to be able to obtain witnesses in one's own behalf for one's defense (Sixth Amendment);   to be confronted with witnesses against one (Sixth Amendment);  to have the right to an attorney (Sixth Amendment); and to be exempt from "cruel or unusual" punishments (Eighth Amendment).  Any state legal system must conform to these safeguards, since the Fourteenth Amendment has extended the guarantee of "due process" to the states.  A large body of criminal law has grown up to define these safeguards.

You cannot be deprived of life, liberty, or property without "due process of law," and some laws applying to minors do not apply to adults.

*Under what conditions can minors be treated differently from adults?*

First, a minor under fourteen is not legally capable of committing a crime and cannot be tried or punished for breaking a law. (Minn. Stat. §609.055) However, a person under the age of fourteen may be found to be a "delinquent child." (Minn. Stat. §260.015) After the age of eighteen, a person is legally an adult and the adult criminal law applies.  Between the ages of fourteen and eighteen a person might be found delinquent and treated as younger children are in the juvenile system, or that person might be referred to the adult court system for prosecution. (Minn. Stat. §260.11) If the person is not referred to the adult court system, a crime has not been committed. (Minn. Stat. §260.215)  Whether or not the person will be referred will be discussed later in this chapter.  Generally adults and children have the same constitutional rights, and the following procedures apply unless otherwise noted.

*Suppose a crime has been committed and a police officer suspects I was involved.  Can I be arrested?*

If the officer saw you commit an offense you can be taken into custody. (Minn. Stat. §260.165)  No child shall be taken into custody except:

**1.** with an order issued by the court after a petition has been filed.

**2.** in accordance with the law pertaining to arrests.

**3.** by a peace officer—when the child has run away from his or her parent or guardian, or when the peace officer reasonably believes the child has run away; when a child is found in surroundings that endanger the health or welfare of that child, or that the officer reasonably believes endangers the child's health or welfare; and when the officer reasonably believes the child has violated terms of any probation or other supervision.

*Can the officer question me with reference to that crime?*

If the officer suspects you might be the person who committed the offense, you cannot be questioned about it until you have been warned of your rights. The warning must show you are a suspect, that anything you say may be used against you in a court proceeding, that you have a right to remain silent, that you have the right to an attorney's advice, and that if you cannot afford a lawyer, the court will appoint one for you. If you are questioned without these safeguards, your statements may not be used against you in court. (*Miranda v. Arizona*, 384 U.S. 436 (1966)). However, if you volunteer information with no duress applied to you for answers, you have waived your right not to incriminate yourself.

    If the police officer does not see you commit an offense but someone has complained, under oath, that you have done certain acts that constitute a crime and the complaint has been taken before a court for the issuance of an order to take you into custody, the police officer may take you into custody on the authority of the court's order. If the officer does not possess the order but has been told over the police radio that a warrant has been issued for your arrest or detention, you may be taken into custody, but you must be shown the warrant as soon as practicable. If no warrant has been issued but a crime has been committed and the officer has reasonable grounds for believing you committed it, you may be taken into custody.

*Can I be arrested "on suspicion"?*

No. The Minnesota Supreme Court says this is prohibited. (*State v. Mitchell*, 285 Minn. 153, 172 N.W.2d 66 (1969))

*If I am under eighteen when the police officer takes me into custody, is this an arrest?*

No. This means you will have no arrest record and later can say you were never arrested.

*If I am taken into custody, can I be put in jail?*

Minors cannot be kept in the same room in a jail as an adult, but they can be put in a separate room in a jail or police station. (Minn. Stat. §260.175)

*Can my car be seized if I am taken into custody?*

Obviously if you are in custody, the car must be towed to some place where it will be safe. If the officer sees certain evidence that the car is being used in

---

RIGHTS OF A
JUVENILE

1. Right to remain silent.
2. Right to a lawyer if juvenile cannot afford one.
3. Right to a fair hearing (but not a jury trial).
4. Right to a free transcript if juvenile cannot afford one.

*Usually, police can only hold minors in custody for a maximum of forty-eight hours.*

a crime—as, for example, if the officer sees stolen goods in plain sight when you are taken into custody—that evidence might be taken into custody. If the car has been involved in the offense, the police might seek to preserve any such evidence. It is always preferable that the police go to the court to get a warrant for detaining such evidence, explaining why. If there is danger of the evidence being removed, the officer could justify acting without the warrant if the detainment was legal. (*State v. London*, 256 N.W.2d 89 (1977); *State v. Kyles*, 257 N.W.2d 378 (1977); *State v. Ray*, 265 N.W.2d 663 (1978); *State v. Turner*, 307 Minn. 284, 230 N.W.2d 468 (1976))

*Must an officer tell me why I am being taken into custody?*

Yes, and if you are under eighteen, your parents must also be informed. (Minn. Stat. §260.171)

*How long can I be held in custody?*

You cannot be held for more than twenty-four hours (excluding Saturdays, Sundays, or holidays) unless an order for your detention specifying the reasons for the order and signed by the judge is issued. You cannot be held for more than thirty-six hours unless a petition is filed to have you declared a delinquent by the court and the judge determines you should remain in custody. (Minn. Stat. §260.171)

*What is the juvenile court?*

Usually the *juvenile court* is not in a separate building from other courts and often it is not a separate judge. It is a system of rules judges use when minors break the law, when minors are neglected, or when they need various protective services. In most counties of the state, a county judge acts as a juvenile judge. In Hennepin and Ramsey Counties the district court is the juvenile court and the chief judge may designate one of the district court judges to hear juvenile matters for a six-year period. (Minn. Stat. §260.019) In other counties the procedure may be different. For example, the chief county judge in St. Louis County selects one judge who hears juvenile matters at Duluth, Hibbing, and Virginia. (Minn. Stat. §260.022) The juvenile court has initial jurisdiction over all accusations of delinquency, juvenile traffic offenders, neglected children, and dependent children. The court also has jurisdiction over adoptions, termination of parental rights (if parents have failed to give the child proper care or protection, or if the parents are unfit), and the appointment of a guardian for children when the parental rights have been terminated. This court must also give consent to marriages when the girl to be married is between sixteen and eighteen years of age. (Minn. Stat. §260.11)

*Why is there a separate court or a special set of rules for juveniles?*

The juvenile court was set up so that the problems of minors could be treated informally and privately. There was also a need for a court that could help children and parents settle family problems in a peaceful way. The law establishing juvenile court says its purpose is to:

> Secure for each minor under the jurisdiction of the court the care and guidance, preferably in his own home, as well as serve the spiritual, emotional, mental and physical welfare of the minor and the best interests of the state; to preserve and strengthen the minor's family ties whenever possible; removing him from custody of his parents only when his welfare or safety and the protection of the public cannot be adequately safeguarded without removal; and when the minor is removed from his own family, to secure for him custody, care and discipline as nearly as possible equivalent to that which should have been given by his parents. (Minn. Stat. §260.011)

(See also the section on neglected or dependent children in Chapter 3.)

*When can a judge terminate parental rights?*

Usually this is the last resort.  As we have seen in the law setting up the juvenile court, the presumption is that a natural parent is fit, and it is in the best interests of the child to be brought up by that parent.  In a case where a child had been in a foster home from the age of eighteen months to nine years, and the mother had had no contact with the child for four years but opposed termination of her parental rights at the hearing, a juvenile court terminated her rights.  But the Minnesota Supreme Court, on appeal, said the court could not terminate her rights for the reasons given—that it was in the best interests of the child.  (*In re Lindgren*, 280 N.W.2d 29 (1979))  The court said there must also be one of the other grounds specified in the law: abandonment; refusal to give the child necessary care and protection though financially able; parental failure to provide necessary care for health, morals, and so forth; parent's habitual use of drugs or intoxicants; parental conduct found by the court to be detrimental to the health or morals of the child; parental failure to correct conditions after a determination of neglect or dependency was determined.

A child may be found to be neglected, even if parental rights are not terminated, and legal custody may be transferred to someone else.

*What is a delinquent child?*

A delinquent child is a person under eighteen who has violated a federal law, any state law, or any local ordinance except a traffic ordinance;  who is a habitual truant, in other words one who is "uncontrolled by the parent, by reason of being wayward or habitually disobedient."  (Minn. Stat. §260.015(5))

*What happens if I am charged with being delinquent?*

Of course, if a police officer observes you break the law you can be taken into custody immediately  (Minn. Stat. §260.165), but your parents must be notified immediately.  (Minn. Stat. §260.171)  If a petition is filed to have you declared a delinquent by the court, a date will be set for hearing on the petition.  You and your parents must have notice of the hearing and you must be told why the hearing is to be held.  Your parents might be required to sign a written promise to return you for the hearing.  Usually, unless there is reason to believe you would endanger yourself or some other person, you will be released until the hearing, either to your parent or some other suitable person.  (Minn. Stat. §260.171)  You may have an attorney represent you at the hearing, and one will be appointed for you without charge if there is an accusation that you have broken a law or if you might be kept overnight.  At a trial, delinquency must be proved "beyond a reasonable doubt" as in a criminal case.  (*In re Winship*, 397 U.S. 358 (1970))

If the offense you are charged with is minor, you might be warned and sent home, but if there is any possibility you might be detained, then there is a hearing and it is necessary to be represented by an attorney.  This has been true since 1967 after the decision by the U.S. Supreme Court in *In re Gault*, 387 U.S. 1.

In that case Gerald Gault was charged with making obscene phone calls, and he admitted he had done it when questioned by the police. The police had not told him he had a right to refuse to answer their questions, or that he had a right to a lawyer, or that he might be confined to a state training school until he was twenty-one. (The case took place before the age of majority was reduced to eighteen years.) The penalty for an adult who had made the same type of call would have been sixty days in jail or a fine of fifty dollars. The court held that such disparity was a violation of Gerald's rights and he was released. Among other things, the U.S. Supreme Court said, "The condition of being a boy does not justify a kangaroo court."

In Minnesota, if a juvenile court decides that a juvenile is not suitable for treatment under the juvenile system, or that the public safety would be endangered by detaining him or her under the juvenile system, an alleged violation of a statute may be referred for prosecution as if the offender were an adult. (*State v. Duncan*, 250 N.W.2d 189 (1977)) (Minn. Stat. §260.125)

California had a similar provision in its juvenile court law. Jones, a seventeen-year-old armed with a dangerous weapon, committed an offense that would be robbery if committed by an adult. He was detained in a juvenile detention home until a hearing at which the court found the alleged facts were true, but the judge continued (postponed) the case for two weeks before deciding what disposition to make of the case. Two weeks later, the judge decided to refer the matter to the adult court system on the grounds that Jones was not amenable to the treatment and training programs available to the juvenile court. Jones's lawyer complained he had had no notice this was to be a "fitness" hearing, and the judge continued the case another week to consider a report of a juvenile officer. Then Jones charged he was being put in double jeopardy for the same offense—he had already been found guilty in effect, and this second trial violated federal and state constitutions. He was held for trial in the adult court anyway, and was found guilty of robbery while armed with a dangerous weapon, and he renewed his claim of "double jeopardy." The state contended he was only being punished once, so could not complain. After appeals in the California court system, the case was appealed to the U.S. Supreme Court, and that court held "jeopardy" was risk—and that the two trials did violate the prohibition against being twice in jeopardy for the same offense, even though there would be but one punishment. The Court said,

> Although the Juvenile Court system had its genesis in a desire to provide a distinctive procedure and setting to deal with the problems of youth . . . our decisions in recent years have recognized there is a gap between the original benign conception of the system and the realities. . . . The Court's response to that perception has been to make applicable in juvenile proceedings constitutional guarantees associated with criminal prosecutions. . . . We believe it is simply too late to conclude that the juvenile is not in jeopardy at a proceeding whose object is to determine whether he has committed acts that violate the criminal law. . . . Here there was no difference between the adjudicatory proceeding and a criminal trial.

The Court also said that if there was to be an exception to the rule against double jeopardy it must be justified either by the interests of society or the juvenile. "We require only that a state determine whether it wants to try a juvenile justice system before entering on a proceeding that may result in an adjudication that he has violated a criminal law and in a substantial deprivation of liberty, rather than to subject him to the expense, delay, strain and embarassment [*sic*] of two proceedings." (*Breed v. Jones*, 421 U.S. 519 (1975))

The Minnesota Supreme Court considered several appeals then pending and in 1976 (*In re Welfare IQS*, 309 Minn. 78, 244 N.W.2d 30) set out the advantages of being treated in the juvenile court, such as many programs functioning in community agencies and specific work or training programs. It pointed out that either the prosecution or the juvenile could appeal a decision of the juvenile court to the Minnesota Supreme Court. Thus, to some extent, it is up to the prosecution to ask for a trial in the adult court system. Also, the juvenile court could waive jurisdiction in those cases that it wished to have heard in regular criminal courts. It must hold a hearing on the question of whether or not it will waive jurisdiction, and the juvenile may be represented by an attorney at that hearing. Much of the proceedings of the juvenile court has been confidential but the juvenile's attorney must be given access to the "social record" of the juvenile. If jurisdiction is waived, the juvenile must be given a statement of the reasons for the waiver. Also, the court pointed out that the entire juvenile system involved a waiver of some rights, such as the right to trial by jury, in return for other rights, such as secrecy of juvenile proceedings, but said any juvenile not wishing to avail himself or herself of this treatment could certainly demand the constitutional right to a trial by jury.

The reasons a court may consider in referring the case (waiving its jurisdiction) are the presence or absence of facilities to treat the juvenile within the system, whether there is a threat to public safety if the juvenile is kept in the juvenile system, and whether the juvenile is amenable to treatment. (*State v. Duncan*, 250 N.W.2d 189) (Minn. Stat. §260.185)

*What happens if the judge retains the case in juvenile court?*

If a judge retains jurisdiction, you are given a hearing on the offense charged, and this must be proved beyond a reasonable doubt. If you are found to have committed the offense, the judge may:

1. Counsel you or your parents or guardian

2. Place you under the supervision of a probation officer or other suitable person in your own home under conditions prescribed by the court, including suitable rules of conduct for you and your parents

3. With the consent of the commissioner of Corrections, place you in a group foster care facility under the supervision of the commissioner

4. Transfer your legal custody to the County Welfare Board, or a child placement agency, or a reputable individual of good moral character

5. Transfer legal custody to a County Home School

6. Transfer legal custody to a county probation officer for placement in a licensed foster home

7. Transfer your custody to the commissioner of Corrections.

If you have destroyed or damaged property, the court may require you to make reasonable restitution. If it thinks it in your best interests and of the public safety, it may recommend to the commissioner of Transportation that your driver's license be cancelled for a period not to exceed the period before your eighteenth birthday.

Any disposition must contain written findings to support whatever disposition the court orders, with the reason for believing this disposition best serves your interests and what alternatives were considered and why such alternatives were not thought to be appropriate.

*How does the judge decide which of these things to do?*

Before deciding, the judge will order an investigation of your home life and background and may order a mental or physical examination. The judge will also hold a hearing to decide what course of treatment is best. (Minn. Stat. §260.151, Minn. J.C.R. 6-1 through 6-7) If you are put on probation, the order will be reconsidered once a year until you are of age (Minn. Stat. §260.185), or unless you are discharged earlier.

If a juvenile has been committed to the commissioner of Corrections, the juvenile court has no further jurisdiction and the commissioner of Corrections may order you confined to the State Training School for Boys, the Minnesota Home School, a group foster home under the control of the commissioner, or to private schools or institutions established to care for delinquent children, or order your release under specified conditions, or discharge you when it has been determined that you have been rehabilitated and your discharge poses no danger to the public. If the commissioner believes you are eligible for probation but your home conditions are not conducive to your continued law-abiding conduct, you may be referred to a child placement agency or the county welfare board for placement in a foster home. After you have been committed to the commissioner, he or she alone has the power to decide on your release. (*Welfare M.D.A. v. State*, 306 Minn. 370, 237 N.W.2d 827 (1975))

*What can I do if I think the judge made a mistake?*

You should consult with your attorney. If there is new evidence, the court might be asked to have another hearing. If there is no new trial but you feel the judge did not follow the law, or that the law infringes on your rights, your attorney may appeal to the state supreme court. The state supreme court ordinarily will not disturb a factual decision unless it is clearly without support in the evidence, but it can decide if a law was misapplied, or if there was a mistake in the conduct of the case. (Minn. Stat. §260.291)

# TRAFFIC

*What is a juvenile traffic offender?*

A juvenile traffic offender is any person under the age of eighteen who violates a state traffic law or local traffic ordinance or who violates a "water traffic" (boating safety) law.  If you are a juvenile traffic offender, you may not be found delinquent, but the same procedures and rules are used as in a delinquency case.  (Minn. Stat. §260.193)

*What can the judge do if it is found that I have broken a traffic law?*

Before making any disposition, the court shall obtain from the Department of Transportation information of any previous traffic violation. (Minn. Stat. §260.193)  Then it may reprimand you and counsel you and your parents, continue the case under conditions for your operation of the vehicle for a reasonable period, require you to attend a driver improvement school, recommend suspension of your driver's license, and if you have had two moving highway violations or have contributed to an accident involving death or injury or damage in excess of $100, recommend cancellation of your license until you are eighteen years old.  The commissioner of Public Safety is authorized to cancel your license without a hearing on such recommendation.  The court may also place you under probation in your own home under reasonable rules relating to the operation of vehicles.  At any time before the period of cancellation of a license has expired, the court may recommend the return of the license and in that case the licensing officer is authorized to return the license.

# CRIMINAL PROCEDURE

*When can a person be arrested?*

If there is no warrant for a person's arrest, an officer may arrest anyone for an offense committed in the officer's presence, or if the officer has reasonable cause to believe a felony was committed and the arrested person committed it.  When a charge has been made upon reasonable cause by someone else to the officer that a felony was committed and the arrested person committed it, the officer may also make an arrest without a warrant.  (Minn. Stat. §629.34)

An officer may arrest a person without a warrant at the arrested person's residence if the peace officer has probable cause to believe that within the past four hours the person arrested has assaulted his or her spouse or any other person living at the residence, although the assault did not take place in the presence of the officer.  The peace officer must first see some physical injury or impairment of the alleged victim to make such an arrest.  (Minn. Stat. §629.341)

If a warrant has been issued for the person's arrest, the officer proceeds as directed by the warrant, and the arrested person has a right to see the warrant.  (Minn. Stat. §629.30)  If the officer does not possess the warrant, it

*A juvenile taken into custody is fingerprinted.*

must be shown to the person arrested as soon as possible after the arrest. (Minn. Stat. §629.32)

*What is a warrant?*

A warrant is a paper signed by a judge directing an officer to arrest a certain person, named or described so as to identify the person, or, if it is a "search warrant," to take into custody certain things described in the warrant.

## FIGURE 5-1  Delinquency Petition

| State of Minnesota<br>Second Judicial District<br>Form JC-24 1-81 | **DELINQUENCY PETITION**<br>**to**<br>**RAMSEY COUNTY JUVENILE COURT** | Intake and Court Use Only:<br><br>Court File No. ___________ |
|---|---|---|

Date Filed Court ___________

Date Initial Appr. ___________

In the Matter of the Welfare of

☐ Active   ☐ Non-Active
Probation Office ___________

_______________   _______________   _______________   _______________
(first)   (middle)   (last)   (date of birth)

Intake Case No. ___________

Child's parents, guardian, spouse or nearest relative, noting their relationship and addresses are as follows:

Date Filed Intake ___________

- - - - - - - - - - - - - - - - - - - - - - - - - - - - - - - - - - - - - - - - - - - - - - - - - - -

A. The specific statutory reference for the law(s) alleged to be violated by the child is(are) as follows:

B. The alleged offense(s), if committed by an adult would be considered:
☐ a Felony   ☐ a Non-Felony   ☐ not applicable

C. Petitioner, being duly sworn, states to the Court and swears to the best of his/her knowledge and belief that said child has committed the following described offenses and that the attached reports or exhibits, consisting of_______ pages, are true and correct and establish probable cause for said belief:

- - - - - - - - - - - - - - - - - - - - - - - - - - - - - - - - - - - - - - - - - - - - - - - - - - -

WHEREFORE, Petitioner requests that said child be brought before the Juvenile Court to be dealt with according to law.

Subscribed and sworn to before me on

_______________   _______________________   _______________________
Date           Notary Public           Petitioner

This petition has been drafted under my supervision and I believe that reasonable grounds exist to support the allegations.

_______________________________   _______________
Ramsey County Attorney         Date

*If I am arrested must I be jailed?*

Not necessarily. You must be taken promptly to a magistrate or judicial officer; you will be told when to appear in court and upon your promise to appear, you may be released, with or without bail.

*Is the court appearance a trial?*

No. At the first appearance, the charge against you is read and you must also receive a copy of the charge or accusation. If the charge is a felony, you must appear in person, but if it is not, your attorney may appear instead. At this appearance, if you have no attorney and may be punished by imprisonment, the court will ask you if you have an attorney and if you can afford an attorney. You must also be told that an attorney will be appointed for you if you are unable to afford one. (Minn. Stat. §630.10) At this time you might be asked whether you plead guilty or not guilty and if you request it, you are given a day to decide. If you make no plea, a "not guilty" plea is entered.

*How long after this appearance am I put on trial?*

The Constitution says you are entitled to a "speedy trial," ordinarily sixty days. (Minn. R. Crim. P. 6.06, 11.10, see also Rule 13) The defendant may want a delay to have time to prepare a defense. If you ask for a delay, you cannot complain that the trial is not "speedy" enough. Also, if there is a possibility of imprisonment if you are convicted, you may ask for a jury trial. These are matters your attorney will decide.

*What is the grand jury?*

Grand jury → Indictment/ No Bill

Petit jury → Guilty/Not Guilty

It is a body of citizens of the county chosen by lot, consisting of not more than twenty-three persons nor fewer than sixteen persons (Minn. Stat. §628.41) whose duty it is to inquire into conditions of all persons imprisoned on criminal charges in the county and into the willful and corrupt misconduct in offices of all the public officers in the county. (Minn. Stat. §628.61) Proceedings of the grand jury are secret; the grand jury is not a trial jury but determines, from the evidence brought before it, whether a person should be charged with a crime or indicted. An *indictment* is an accusation in writing. The grand jury decides from the evidence before it, unless explained or contradicted, whether a person is guilty of a crime and, if so, brings this indictment.

*Must all accusations of crime be brought before a grand jury?*

No. An offense that may be punished by life imprisonment must be prosecuted after indictment by a grand jury. (U.S. Const. Amendment V) Any other offense may be prosecuted either on an indictment or filing of a complaint, which is made under oath before a judicial officer. The complaint must give the facts establishing probable cause that a crime was committed and that the defendant committed it. If the complaint is taken from oral, sworn testimony, that testimony must be reduced to writing. A complaint is not filed unless the prosecuting attorney approves it—except that if the prosecutor is unavailable and the judge certifies that fact and the fact that the issuance of the complaint should not be delayed, it may be issued.

If the offense is a misdemeanor, the defendant may be ordered into court on a tab charge instead of a complaint, with a brief statement of the offense charged.  (Minn. R. Crim. P. 2, 4)

*What does the prosecutor have to tell the defense before trial?*

The prosecutor must disclose names of witnesses who will be called, the physical evidence that will be used, reports of any tests, and physical or mental examinations.  The prosecutor must also disclose any prior criminal conviction.  If the prosecutor knows any fact that might reduce the degree of crime, that fact must be disclosed.  The defense has a duty to disclose names of defense witnesses or prior criminal record.  If it appears that introduction of any of the proposed evidence would endanger a defendant's rights, he or she may ask for a hearing before the trial as to whether this specific testimony should be admitted.

*What is a speedy trial?*

On written demand, the trial shall start within sixty days from demand unless "for good cause shown" the trial cannot be held then. (MN Rules Crim. Proc. 11)  The sixty days begins after the defendant has entered a plea of not guilty and demanded immediate hearing.  (Minn. R. Crim. P. 11.10)

*If the accused demands a jury trial, who selects the jury?*

The jurors are drawn by lot from the citizens of the county.  People in certain occupations are excused from service, and elderly, disabled, or people who do not speak or understand English may be excused.  At the beginning of the trial, jurors are questioned first by the judge, then by each attorney.  If a juror is even distantly related to the complainant or the accused, has previously sued the defendant in an unrelated civil matter, or has been otherwise connected with either party in some business transaction, he or she may be challenged for bias or cause.  In addition, if the offense may be punished by life imprisonment, the defense has fifteen "peremptory" challenges and the state has nine "peremptory" challenges.  These challenges are used to strike from the jury panel members who the respective attorneys feel uncomfortable with, even though the prospective juror does not fit one of the types of "cause" for disqualification.  If the possible punishment is less than life, the defense has five peremptory challenges and the prosecution has three.

*If I am entitled to a jury of my peers, may I insist on jurors of my own age or social class?*

No.  Jurors are to be a cross section of the population and they must be over eighteen years of age and residents of the county.  Unless there is a systematic exclusion of any particular group, a random selection of jurors meets the requirement of a jury of your peers.

*Must a person be present at a trial on a felony or misdemeanor?*

Generally yes, but if the accused leaves the state while on bail, he or she can be tried in his or her absence. (*State ex rel Shetsky v. Utecht*, 228 Minn. 44, 36 N.W.2d 126, 6 ALR 2d 988 (1949))

Also, if a defendant is boisterous or disorderly after being warned by the court, the court may order him or her removed until the verdict is read. (Minn. Stat. §631.015)

*Can a person be punished for his or her conduct in a courtroom?*

Yes. All courts have an inherent right to punish contempt committed in their presence. (Minn. Stat. §588.02)  This rule applies to juvenile courts as well as other courts.

OATH TO WITNESSES
"You do swear that the evidence you shall give relative to the cause now under consideration shall be the whole truth, and nothing but the truth. So help you God."

*May I refuse to testify in response to a subpoena?*

No.  This would be contempt of court.

*What if I feel the testimony might incriminate me?*

Then you might be excused.  However, if the testimony is in reference to a civil matter and you are not going to be tried as a criminal, you may not refuse to answer.

*What happens if I give false answers in court?*

You may be guilty of perjury  (Minn. Stat. §609.48) and be subject to five years imprisonment or a fine of $5,000.

*What can happen if I threaten a person who may testify against me with harm, or threaten harm to that person's family if the testimony is given?*

This is tampering with a witness, punishable by imprisonment of up to five years or a fine of up to $5,000.  (Minn. Stat. §609.498)

*May a person be convicted for more than one offense arising out of the same circumstances?*

Not if it arises out of the same "behavioral incident." (Minn. Stat. §609.035) However, a person may be convicted for burglary (entry by illegal means with intent to commit a crime) and for the crime committed after the illegal entry. (Minn. Stat. §609.585) (*State v. Alexander*, Jan. 11, 1980)

*What happens to a person convicted of a crime?*

The statutes provide certain maximum punishments for each crime.  Unless the conviction is for a felony requiring a life sentence, the court may order a presentence investigation into the defendant's individual characteristics, circumstances, needs, potentialities, criminal record, and social history. After this, he or she may be sentenced for a term not to exceed the statutory maximum, or impose a fine not to exceed the statutory maximum (if this is provided for that crime), or both. If the sentence is for more than one year, the prisoner is sentenced to the commissioner of Corrections, who may determine where the time shall be served. (Minn. Stat. §609.10) If the sentence is for less than a year, the judge may direct that the time be served in a workhouse, county jail, or other facility. However, if the statute directs that the minimum sentence must be for more than one year, as it is even in a first conviction when a dangerous weapon is used, the judge may not direct that the time be served in a local facility (*State v. Jonason* and *State v. Olson* 3-14-80), and the prisoner may not be placed on probation.

Effective May 1, 1980, sentencing guidelines were established that are designed to make sentences more uniform throughout the state for persons in similar circumstances. When a person is convicted of a felony, the court must hold a separate hearing at which all factors bearing on the appropriateness of a sentence may be presented. If a court departs from the guidelines, the judge must make written findings indicating why it did so.

*If a person is sentenced to imprisonment for a term of years, must he or she serve that time?*

Not always. Except when a sentence to life imprisonment is required by law, a court may "stay" the imposition or execution of a sentence and place the defendant on probation on such conditions as the court may prescribe. The court may order probation under supervision of a probation officer of the court, or if there is none and the offense is a felony, probation by the commissioner of Corrections. If a stay is granted, it cannot exceed the term of the sentence that could have been imposed for the offense. If the convicted person does nothing to cause the stay to be revoked until the end of the term, he or she is discharged. (Minn. Stat. §609.135)

If a defendant violates the terms of the stay or is guilty of misconduct, the court may revoke the stay and direct that he or she be taken into custody. The prisoner is entitled, however, to written notice of the revocation and if he or she disputes the grounds, a hearing on that issue is given. (Minn. Stat. §609.14)

Any prisoner may earn a reduction of up to one-third of the sentence by not being involved in any violation of prison rules or disciplinary offense. Also, the commissioner of Corrections must inform a prisoner of the scope of the mutual agreement programs and if the prisoner desires one, a program may be drafted with provision for vocational or educational training. Participation in the program may not affect the length of the sentence, but it may make it possible for part of the sentence to be served in some facility less restrictive than a prison. Also, the Board of Corrections, on recommendation of the commissioner of Corrections, may release prisoners for various other work programs. To be released, the prisoner must have served half the sentence, less the time earned for good behavior, and, during the release, he or she may be housed in some local institution. (Minn. Stat. §241.26) Willful failure to abide by the conditions of these release programs is grounds for revoking this provisional release.

*If a delinquent child is committed to the commissioner of Corrections, is he or she placed in a penal institution?*

Not if committed by the juvenile court.  (Minn. Stat. §§242.14 and 242.18)

*Can murderers be paroled?*

Yes.  If they are serving a term of life imprisonment, they may not be paroled until they have served twenty years, less time off for good behavior.  (Minn. Stat. §243.05)

*Who decides whether a prisoner should be paroled?*

The corrections board, which consists of five members, four appointed by the governor with the consent of the Senate and a chairman who is an officer of the Department of Corrections appointed by the commissioner of Corrections to serve at the commissioner's pleasure. (Minn. Stat. §241.045) This board decides questions of granting or revoking paroles and issuing final discharges to people who have earned such right. For a fuller discussion of the rights of the accused, see Appendix B.


## SENTENCING GUIDELINES

The guidelines to sentencing take into consideration a convict's "criminal history" as well as the seriousness of the crime.  In the following table the vertical column at left lists crimes in order of seriousness from I to X and the criminal history runs horizontally from 0 to 6.  Some time in the institution is required under the heavy diagonal line.  Otherwise, sentences are given in months.  In computing the criminal history sentences for felonies that expired ten years or more before the present offense are ignored if there was no further brush with the law in the interim, and the misdemeanor convictions are ignored if more than five years have passed without trouble since expiration of the sentence.  Only misdemeanors under state statutes and felonies are considered—not minor traffic offenses.  A misdemeanor violation counts only one unit toward the four units making a point on the scale, so four misdemeanor violations might make the difference between a twenty-one-month and twenty-six-month sentence for second degree assault, for example.  Gross misdemeanors count for two units, and felony convictions for one point. Juvenile adjudictions of delinquency for offenses that would be felonies if committed by an adult and that were committed after the delinquent was sixteen are counted, but at the rate of one point for two offenses, which would have been felonies if committed by an adult.

From Tables 5-2, 5-3, 5-4, 5-5, and 5-6 you should be able to compute the presumptive sentences for various types of situations.  But remember, a judge may depart from the guidelines if written reasons for doing so are filed.

**TABLE 5-2   Sentencing Guidelines in Months†**

CRIMINAL HISTORY SCORE

| SEVERITY LEVELS OF CONVICTION OFFENSE | | 0 | 1 | 2 | 3 | 4 | 5 | 6 or more |
|---|---|---|---|---|---|---|---|---|
| *Unauthorized Use of Motor Vehicle* *Possession of Marijuana* | I | 12* | 12* | 12* | 15 | 18 | 21 | 24 |
| *Theft Related Crimes ($150-$2500)* *Sale of Marijuana* | II | 12* | 12* | 14 | 17 | 20 | 23 | 27 <br> 25-29 |
| *Theft Crimes ($150-$2500)* | III | 12* | 13 | 16 | 19 | 22 <br> 21-23 | 27 <br> 25-29 | 32 <br> 30-34 |
| *Burglary-Felony Intent* *Receiving Stolen Goods ($150-$2500)* | IV | 12* | 15 | 18 | 21 | 25 <br> 24-26 | 32 <br> 30-34 | 41 <br> 37-45 |
| *Simple Robbery* | V | 18 | 23 | 27 | 30 <br> 29-31 | 38 <br> 36-40 | 46 <br> 43-49 | 54 <br> 50-58 |
| *Assault, 2nd Degree* | VI | 21 | 26 | 30 | 34 <br> 33-35 | 44 <br> 42-46 | 54 <br> 50-58 | 65 <br> 60-70 |
| *Aggravated Robbery* | VII | 24 <br> 23-25 | 32 <br> 30-34 | 41 <br> 38-44 | 49 <br> 45-53 | 65 <br> 60-70 | 81 <br> 75-87 | 97 <br> 90-104 |
| *Assault, 1st Degree* *Criminal Sexual Conduct,* *1st Degree* | VIII | 43 <br> 41-45 | 54 <br> 50-58 | 65 <br> 60-70 | 76 <br> 71-81 | 95 <br> 89-101 | 113 <br> 106-120 | 132 <br> 124-140 |
| *Murder, 3rd Degree* | IX | 97 <br> 94-100 | 119 <br> 116-122 | 127 <br> 124-130 | 149 <br> 143-155 | 176 <br> 168-184 | 205 <br> 195-215 | 230 <br> 218-242 |
| *Murder, 2rd Degree* | X | 116 <br> 111-121 | 140 <br> 133-147 | 162 <br> 153-171 | 203 <br> 192-214 | 243 <br> 231-255 | 284 <br> 270-298 | 324 <br> 309-339 |

†*Italicized numbers within the table denote the range within which a judge may sentence without the sentence being deemed a departure. First Degree Murder is excluded from the guidelines by law and continues to have a mandatory life sentence.*
*One year and one day.

**TABLE 5-3  Offense Severity**

| X | Murder 2 - 609.19 |
|---|---|

| IX | Murder 3 - 609.195 |
|---|---|

| VIII | Assault 1 - 609.221 |
|---|---|
| | Attempted Murder 1 - 609.185 with 609.17 or 609.175 cited |
| | Criminal Sexual Conduct 1 - 609.342 |
| | Kidnapping (w/great bodily harm) - 609.25, subd. 2(2) |
| | Manslaughter 1 - 609.20(1) & (2) |

| VII | Aggravated Robbery - 609.245 |
|---|---|
| | Arson 1 - 609.561 |
| | Criminal Sexual Conduct 2 - 609.343(c), (d), (e), & (f) |
| | Criminal Sexual Conduct 3 - 609.344(c) & (d) |
| | Kidnapping (not in safe place) - 609.25, subd. 2(2) |
| | Manslaughter 1 - 609.20(3) |
| | Manslaughter 2 - 609.205(1) |

| VI | Arson 2 - 609.562 |
|---|---|
| | Assault 2 - 609.222 |
| | Burglary - 609.58, subd. 2(1)(b) & (2) |
| | Criminal Sexual Conduct 2 - 609.343(a) & (b) |
| | Criminal Sexual Conduct 4 - 609.345(c) & (d) |
| | Escape from Custody - 609.485, subd. 4(4) |
| | Kidnapping - 609.25, subd. 2(1) |
| | Receiving Stolen Goods (over $2,500) - 609.225; 609.53 |
| | Sale of Hallucinogens or PCP - 152.15, subd. 1(2) |
| | Sale of Heroin - 152.15, subd. 1(1) |
| | Sale of Remaining Schedule I & II Narcotics - 152.15, subd. 1(1) |

| V | Criminal Negligence Resulting in Death - 609.21 |
|---|---|
| | Criminal Sexual Conduct 3 - 609.344(b) |
| | Manslaughter 2 - 609.205(2), (3), & (4) |
| | Perjury - 609.48, subd. 4(1) |
| | Possession of Incendiary Device - 299F.80; 299F.815; 299F.811 |
| | Simple Robbery - 609.24 |
| | Solicitation of Prostitution - 609.322, subd. 1 |
| | Tampering w/Witness - 609.498, subd. 1 |

| IV | Assault 3 - 609.223 |
|---|---|
| | Bribery - 609.42; 90.41 |
| | Bring Contraband into State Prison - 243.55 |
| | Bring Dangerous Weapon into County Jail - 641.165, subd. 2(b) |
| | Burglary - 609.58, subd. 2(1)(a), (c), & (3) |
| | Criminal Sexual Conduct 4 - 609.345(b) |
| | Negligent Fires - 609.576(a) |
| | Perjury - 290.53, subd. 4; 300.61; & 609.48, subd. 4(2) |
| | Receiving Profit Derived from Prostitution - 609.323, subd. 1 |
| | Receiving Stolen Goods ($150-$2500) - 609.525; 609.53 |
| | Security Violations (over $2500) - 80A.22, subd. 1; 80B.10, subd. 1; 80C.16, subd. 3(a) & (b) |
| | Terroristic Threats - 609.713, subd. 1 |
| | Theft Crimes - Over $2,500 *(See Theft Offense List)* |
| | Theft from Person - 609.52 |
| | Use of Drugs to Injure or Facilitate Crime - 609.235 |

**TABLE 5-3——**_Continued_

**III**

Aggravated Forgery (over $2,500) - 609.625
Arson 3 - 609.563
Coercion - 609.27, subd. 1(1)
Coercion (over $2,500) - 609.27, subd. 1(2), (3), (4), & (5)
Damage to Property - 609.595, subd. 1(1)
Dangerous Trespass - 609.60;  609.85(1)
Dangerous Weapons - 609.67, subd. 2;  624.713, subd. 1(b)
Escape from Custody - 609.485, subd. 4(1)
False Imprisonment - 609.255
Negligent Discharge of Explosion - 299F.83
Possession of Burglary Tools - 609.59
Possession of Hallucinogens or PCP - 152.15, subd. 2(2)
Possession of Heroin - 152.15, subd. 2(1)
Possession of Remaining Schedule I & II Narcotics - 152.15, subd. 2(1)
Prostitution (Patron) - 609.324, subd. 1
Receiving Profit Derived from Prostitution - 609.323, subd. 2
Sale of Cocaine - 152.15, subd. 1(2)
Sale of Remaining Schedule I, II, & III Non-narcotics - 152.15, subd. 1(2)
Security Violation (under $2500) - 80A.22, subd. 1; 80B.10, subd. 1; 80C.16, subd. 3(a) & (b)
Solicitation of Prostitution - 609.322, subd. 2
Theft Crimes - $150-$2,500 _(See Theft Offense List)_
Theft of Public Records - 609.52
Theft Related Crimes - Over $2,500 _(See Theft Related Offense List)_

**II**

Aggravated Forgery ($150-$2,500) - 609.625
Aggravated Forgery (misc) (non-check) - 609.625;  609.635;  609.64
Coercion ($300-$2,500) - 609.27, subd. 1(2), (3), (4), & (5)
Damage to Property - 609.595, subd. 1(2) & (3)
Negligent Fires (damage greater than $10,000) - 609.576(b)(4)
Riot - 609.71
Sale of Marijuana/Hashish/Tetrahydrocannabinols - 152.15, subd. 1(2)
Sale of Schedule IV Substance - 152.15, subd. 1(3)
Terroristic Threats - 609.713, subd. 2
Theft-Looting - 609.52
Theft Related Crimes - $150-$2,500 _(See Theft Related Offense List)_

**I**

Aggravated Forgery (Less than $150) - 609.625
Aiding Offender to Avoid Arrest - 609.495
Forgery - 609.63;  and Forgery Related Crimes _(See Forgery Related Offense List)_
Fraudulent Procurement of a Controlled Substance - 152.15, subd. 3
Leaving State to Evade Establishment of Paternity - 609.31
Nonsupport of Wife or Child - 609.375, subds. 2, 3, & 4
Possession of Cocaine - 152.15, subd. 2(2)
Possession of Marijuana/Hashish/Tetrahydrocannabinols - 152.15, subd. 2(2)
Possession of Remaining Schedule I, II, & III Non-narcotics - 152.15, subd. 2(2)
Possession of Schedule IV Substance - 152.15, subd. 2(3)
Selling Liquor that Causes Injury - 340.70
Solicitation of Prostitution - 609.322, subd. 3
Unauthorized Use of Motor Vehicle - 609.55

**TABLE 5-4   Theft Offense List**

Altering Serial Number
609.52, Subd. 2(10)(11)

Diversion of Corporate Property
300.60

Embezzlement of Public Funds
609.54

Failure to Pay Over State Funds
609.445

Permitting False Claims Against Government
609.445

Possession of Shoplifting Gear
609.521

Rustling and Livestock Theft
609.551

Theft
609.52, Subd. 2(1)

Theft by Soldier of Military Goods
192.36

Theft by Trick
609.52, Subd. 2(4)

Theft of Public Funds
609.52

Theft of Trade Secret
609.52, Subd. 2(8)

*It is recommended that the above property crimes be treated similarly. This is the list cited for the two THEFT CRIMES ($150—$2,500 and over $2,500) in Table 5-3.*

**TABLE 5-5   Theft-related Offense List**

Defeating Security on Personality
609.62

Defeating Security on Reality
609.615

Defrauding Insurer
609.611

Fraud in Obtaining Credit
609.82

Fraudulent Long Distance Telephone Calls
609.785

Medical Assistance Fraud
609.466

Presenting False Claims to Public Officer or Body
609.465

Refusing to Return Lost Property
609.52, Subd. 2(6)

Taking Pledged Property
609.52, Sub. 2(2)

Temporary Theft
609.52, Subd. 2(5)

Theft by Check
609.52, Subd. 2(3)

Theft of Cable TV Services
609.52, Subd. 2(12)

Theft of Leased Property
609.52, Subd. 2(9)

Unauthorized Use of Credit Card
609.52, Subd. 2(3)

Wrongfully Obtaining Assistance
256.98

*It is recommended that the above property crimes be treated similarly.  This is the list cited for the two*
*THEFT RELATED CRIMES ($150—$2,500 and over $2,500) in Table 5-3.*

**TABLE 5-6   Forgery-related Offense List**

Altering Livestock Certificate
35.824

Altering Packing House Certificate
226.05

Destroy or Falsify Private Business Record
609.63, Subd. 1(5)

Destroy or Falsify Public Record
609.63, Subd. 1(6)

Destroy Writing to Prevent Use at Trial
609.63, 1(7)

False Bill of Lading
228.45;  228.47;  228.49;  228.50;  228.51

False Certification by Notary Public
609.65

False Membership Card
609.63, Subd. 1(3)

False Merchandise Stamp
609.63, Subd. 2(2)

Fraudulent Statements
609.645

Obtaining Signature by False Pretense
609.635

Offer Forged Writing at Trial
609.63, Subd. 2

Recording, Filing of Forged Instrument
609.64

Use of False Identification
609.63, Subd. 1(1)

*It is recommended that the above property crimes be treated similarly.  This is the list cited for the FORGERY and FORGERY RELATED CRIMES in Table 5-3.*

## PROBLEM 1

Dan is sixteen and works as a stock clerk in Mr. Grogan's grocery store. One Saturday night before closing, he slips an extra set of store keys into his pocket. He returns to the store after hours, taking two six-packs of beer, some snack food, and the keys for the store's delivery truck, along with a credit card used to buy gas for the truck. After gasing up and riding around until the early hours of the morning he spots Jim, the guy who beat him out as halfback this fall, driving home from a date. He chases Jim with the truck and tries to run him off the road, but Jim outruns him in his car. Dan returns the truck to the store that morning. Mr. Grogan finds out about Dan's using the truck, fires him on the spot, and says that he will bring in the police. Dan tells him that if he is reported, Dan and his friends will wreck Mr. Grogan's store.

1. What violations of statutes or ordinances did Dan commit?

2. How may these violations be punished?

Now let's add some facts about Dan. He is a senior in high school. He was an average student, but lately his grades have fallen off. He has "mouthed off" to teachers and has aquired a new set of unsavory friends. He ignores his parents and was picked up a month ago for possession of beer. He was fined and given a warning on that violation.

3. If you were the judge, would you permit him to be tried as an adult? Why or why not?

4. Assume you are a member of the Minnesota Corrections Authority. Reception center evaluations of Dan has turned up no significant physical or mental problems. What program would you recommend for Dan?

## PROBLEM 2

Now that you have read the material on the juvenile court, you know that within a framework imposed by the juvenile's rights, the court has a great deal of latitude in deciding what course of action is best for each child.

Pretend for a moment that you are a judge in the juvenile court in your community. How would you decide the following case?

Mary Beth is sixteen and a junior in high school. When she was twelve, her father separated from her mother and now lives in another state. He does not pay support, nor is it likely that if the district court attempted to enforce support he would be able to pay much. Mary Beth and her brother, Steve, age six, appear well-cared for. Their mother obviously cares a great deal about them and is concerned with their situation, but she works to support the family, which takes a great deal of her time.

Mary Beth has been before the court previously.  The first time was for shoplifting a small item when she was fourteen and the last time was when she was returned to her home after running away for six weeks.  This incident occurred right after her father had visited their home and beaten up on the children.

Last night, Mary Beth was spotted by the police wandering around Main Street at 11:30 p.m.  They picked her up for a curfew violation.  The school authorities report that she has been skipping school lately.  The county welfare department has filed a petition to declare her delinquent.

Mary Beth states that she feels no one cares about or understands her.  On the other hand, she says she knows her mother loves her, that she does not want to be taken from the home, and that she will try very hard to stay out of trouble if she is allowed to return home.

1. Should Mary Beth be determined a delinquent child?  What are the alternatives to this determination?

2. If she is determined delinquent, what future course of action should be taken?  If she is not determined delinquent, should the matter be dropped or are there other actions that should be taken?

# 6

# SCHOOL

Everyone knows that the law requires young people to go to school. This chapter will try to explain the rules governing school attendance, the consequences of a failure to attend school, and the kinds of activities within the school that may lead to undesirable consequences.

In general, it might be said that the state has an obligation to furnish a free education to all of its young citizens, that people under a certain age must attend school, and that their parents must allow them to attend school.

While students are in school they are subject to reasonable discipline; if they fail to obey the rules and the offense is serious enough, or if they cause a disruption, they may be suspended for a short period of time or expelled permanently. But students do not lose their rights simply by going to school; the school administration can't be arbitrary and unreasonable in its handling of students.

## CASE STUDY

*Jane and Tom, both fifteen-year-olds and close friends, decide to deface a political poster the social studies teacher has hung on the bulletin board. The*

## CONTENTS

*teacher catches them and, in a fit of anger, kicks them out of the classroom. The principal much later finds them wandering in the halls and, upon questioning, hears the whole story. Jane and Tom say they were protesting the partisan nature of the poster. The teacher insists they both be expelled from school.*

1.  Can the students be suspended?  Expelled?

2.  What should the principal do?

3.  Do students have a right to protest?

4.  If so, how broad is that right?

---

**SELF-QUIZ**

Before you read the chapter, try the following quiz.  Answer each question as best you can, based on your knowledge.  When you have read the chapter, go back to see whether or not you have changed your mind about any of the answers.

1.  Everyone must go to school from the age of five until the age of sixteen. _______ True _______ False

2.  If a student fails to attend school the parents can be convicted of a misdemeanor. _______ True _______ False

3.  A student who refuses to attend school may come under the jurisdiction of the juvenile court. _______ True _______ False

4.  There is no longer any such thing as a truant officer in Minnesota. _______ True _______ False

5.  Because the law requires that everybody attend school, a student may not be expelled permanently for any reason. _______ True _______ False

6.  A student who is exercising the constitutional right of free speech may not be disciplined by the school. _______ True _______ False

7.  Before a student is dismissed from school, he or she is entitled to a hearing. _______ True _______ False

8.  A school may set reasonable standards of dress and hair style. _______ True _______ False

9.  Suspension and expulsion are the same thing. _______ True _______ False

10.  A teacher may never touch a student without the student's permission. _______ True _______ False

11.  School officials can search a student's locker at any time under Minnesota law. _______ True _______ False

# ATTENDANCE

*Do I have to go to school?*

Yes. Everyone between the ages of seven and sixteen must go to school on a regular basis. Schools must meet for at least 175 days in the calendar year. (Minn. Stat. §124.19) However, your parents may request that you be excused from attendance and the local school board may permit it (a) if your health is so poor that you cannot go to school and do your work, (b) if you have already completed all work required in the tenth grade, or (c) if your parents want you to take religious training for up to three hours a week (release time). (Minn. Stat. §120.10)

*Is it all right to go to a private school?*

Yes. This is permitted if the teaching is all done in English (except for language courses) and the teachers have essentially the same qualifications as the teachers in the public schools. (Minn. Stat. §120.10)

*Can my parents set up a school in our home and teach me and my brothers and sisters instead of sending us to the local schools?*

Yes, but it is very difficult to do. The education you receive must be essentially equivalent education to that received in a more formal school setting. Your parents must have essentially the same qualifications as public school teachers. This usually means a highly structured educational setting in the home. The Department of Education is usually reluctant to approve such in-home schools since socializing with others, one of the important factors in education, is missing in such educational settings. (Minn. Stat. §120.10 and Op. Atty. Gen. 160-H May 7, 1941 and Op. Atty. Gen. 169-B Feb. 1, 1944) It is true that the Amish in Wisconsin are permitted by the U.S. Supreme Court to end the formal education of their children after eighth grade, and to educate them in vocational training on the farm since their very way of life is an expression of their religious beliefs. (*Wisconsin v. Yoder*, 406 U.S. 205, 92 S.Ct. 1526, 32 L.Ed. 2d 15 (1972))

*What are the meanings of the terms* in loco parentis *and* parens patriae?

*In loco parentis* is a Latin phrase meaning "in place of the parent;" *parens patriae* means "parent of the country." Historically, teachers have stood in the place of the parent during the school hours so that whatever the parent could legally do to and with the child so could the teacher. This concept has been weakening somewhat in modern times as we will see later in this chapter in the discussion of suspension and expulsion of the student from school. *Parens patriae* refers to the idea that the sovereign power (e.g., the state of Minnesota) has power of guardianship over persons under disability such as minors, the insane, and the incompetent. This concept has been used to justify laws such as compulsory attendance at school, even when the parents do not want the child to attend school.

*What happens if I don't go to school?*

The truant officer may arrest you, even without a warrant, and take you back to school. (Minn. Stat. §120.14) The officer may also order your parents to keep you in school. (Minn. Stat. §120.14)

*Can my parents get in trouble if I don't go to school?*

Yes. The local superintendent of schools may notify your parents that you have been absent without an excuse and order them to send you to school. If they don't do so they are guilty of a misdemeanor and may be prosecuted. (Minn. Stat. §§120.12 and 127.20)

*Do I have to go to school even if I need to work during the day to earn money to live on?*

Yes. If your family is so poor that you must work, and this would interfere with your schooling or keep you out of school completely, you should contact the local school board. They are required to give you financial aid so that you can go to school. (Minn. Stat. §120.16)

*What can happen to me if I refuse to attend school?*

The school boards are allowed to set up special schools for students who are "habitual truants;" who are "incorrigible" (uncontrollable), "vicious," or "immoral;" or who "habitually wander about the streets during school hours." These students are deemed to be delinquent and the school board may require them to go to truant school or bring them before the juvenile court for "discipline." (Minn. Stat. §120.15) The state law does not specifically define "habitual truant" or say how many days you may cut

*Are there any stores near your school that post signs like this?*

school before being classified as a habitual truant. Usually "habitual" means that something is done very often. Whether or not a student is a habitual truant is decided according to the facts of each individual case by the school board or by a court.

*What can the juvenile court do to me if I am found to be a habitual truant?*

Any habitual truant can be declared a "delinquent child" by the juvenile court. The judge can then do whichever of the following things is deemed best for you:

**1.** Counsel with you and your parents.

**2.** Place you under the supervision of a probation officer at home or put you in a group foster home.

**3.** Take custody from your parents and transfer it to a child placement agency, the county welfare board, another person (usually a relative), a county home school, or a group foster home.

**4.** Take custody from your parents and transfer it to the Minnesota Corrections Authority. (Minn. Stat. §§ 260.185 and .191)

What the court actually does in any case depends on such things as the reason that you missed school, the attitude of your parents, the nature of your home life, and any special problems you might have. Prior to making a decision, the court would have a hearing on all of these issues and might also order an investigation of all the facts and circumstances. (For more information, see the section on juvenile court in Chapter 5.)

## SUSPENSION, EXCLUSION, AND EXPULSION

*What is the difference between being suspended, excluded, and expelled from school?*

*Suspension* means an action taken by the school administration, under rules promulgated by the school board, prohibiting a pupil from attending school for a period of no more than five days. This definition does not apply to dismissal from school for one school day or less. (Minn. Stat. §127.27 subd. 10) Minnesota refuses to call a one-day-or-less removal a suspension. But the U.S. Supreme Court has implied that even a one-day removal might be a suspension. (*Goss v. Lopez*, 419 U.S. 565 (1975)) *Exclusion* means an action taken by the school board to prevent enrollment or reenrollment of a pupil for a period that shall not extend beyond the school year. (Minn. Stat. §127.27 subd. 4) *Expulsion* means an action taken by a school board to prohibit an enrolled pupil from further attendance for a period that shall not extend beyond the school year. (Minn. Stat. §127.27 subd. 5) Therefore, the difference between exclusion and expulsion is that a presently enrolled student is expelled, whereas a student seeking enrollment is excluded.

*For what reasons can I be suspended, excluded, or expelled from school?*

According to the Pupil Fair Dismissal Act of 1974 (Minn. Stat. §§127.26 to 127.39), a student can be suspended, excluded, or expelled from school for any of the following actions:

**1.** Willful violation of any reasonably known and definite school board regulation to which students must conform their conduct.

**2.** Willful conduct that materially or substantially disrupts the rights of others to an education.

**3.** Willful conduct that endangers the pupil or other pupils, or the property of the school.

Some of the more interesting decisions involving suspension or expulsion include the following cases. A student who has a contagious disease may be temporarily suspended from school because of the health hazard to the other students. (*Bright v. Beard*, 132 Minn. 375, 157 N.W. 501 (1916)) A student who is caught smoking in violation of the law outside the school grounds may not be expelled. Students cannot be expelled simply because they are married. (Op.Atty.Gen., 169-i May 1, 1965) One federal court decided that a male high school student could not be expelled from a Minnesota public school simply because he had shoulder-length hair. The court said that the student had the right to wear the hair style of his choice because the school could not show his hair was a health hazard or that it would substantially interfere with school discipline. (*Westley v. Rossi*, 305 F. Supp. 706 (Minn. 1969))

The important thing to remember is that you can be suspended, excluded, or expelled if you have done something that causes a danger to the health of the other students or that seriously interferes with order and discipline in the school.

*What rights do I have in a suspension, exclusion, or expulsion proceeding?*

Minnesota grants differing rights depending on the type of proceeding being used. If the student is being suspended for one day or less, the Minnesota Pupil Fair Dismissal Act of 1974 grants no procedural rights because the law says suspension does not apply to dismissal from school for one school day or less. (Minn. Stat. 127.27 subd. 10) But *Goss v. Lopez* (419 U.S. 565 (1975)) stated that it is unconstitutional for a student to be suspended for ten days or less without a hearing. The Court stated that when students have a state right to an education, that right may not be taken away without due process of law (see Appendix B for a detailed discussion of due process).

If the suspension is for more than one day but no more than five school days, then before the suspension an informal conference with the pupil is required (except where it appears that the pupil will create an immediate and substantial danger to other persons or property). Also a written notice containing the grounds for the suspension, a brief statement of the facts, a description of the testimony, a readmission plan, and a copy of the Pupil Fair Dismissal Act must be given to the pupil and the parents or guardian at least forty-eight hours before the informal conference with the administration of the school. (Minn. Stat. §127.30)

If a pupil is to be suspended for more than five days, then this is an expulsion. In an expulsion the procedures are much more stringent. The law says that no expulsion shall be imposed without a hearing unless the hearing is given up by the pupil and parent or guardian. At the hearing, the pupil has many rights such as the right to written notice detailing a complete statement of facts, list of witnesses and description of their testimony, the right to have legal counsel at the hearing, and the right to present evidence and cross-examine witnesses. (Minn. Stat. §127.31) The same is true for an exclusion.

*Do I have any rights if I am excluded or expelled from school?*

Even if after a hearing you are excluded or expelled, the dismissal can only last until the end of the school year. So that the next year you can reenroll and the only way the school can exclude you is if you have another full hearing. Also, during the time you are excluded or expelled the school district has a continuing responsibility to educate you and help you prepare for read-mission. (Minn. Stat. §127.38) This could mean a private tutor would have to be provided and paid for by the school district.

*What can I do if I'm expelled and I don't think there was a good reason?*

Your parents could take additional legal action to get you back in school. Your parents could ask for an *injunction*. This is an order from the court that prohibits somebody else from doing something. In this kind of case, the school would be prohibited by the court from dismissing you if their reasons for doing so did not conform to the law or if they failed to extend to your legal rights.

## DEMONSTRATIONS AND PROTEST

*Can I be expelled from school for demonstrating or protesting?*

This is a very complicated problem; it is not simply a question of Minnesota law but involves the Constitution of the United States. The First Amendment to the Constitution guarantees the right of free speech to all citizens (including students), but there are often problems about what is really speech and what is really an act. Also the right of free speech is not absolute: you can't, to use a famous expression, yell "fire" in a crowded theater and not be punished for it.

The U.S. Supreme Court decided one case involving student protests in school that is interesting. Two high school students and one junior high school student who had worn black armbands to school to protest the war in Vietnam were suspended. The Court said that the school was wrong to

"Congress shall make no law respecting an establishment of religion, or prohibiting the free exercise thereof; or abridging the freedom of speech, or of the press; or the right of the people peacably to assemble, and to petition the government for a redress of grievances."——*First Amendment, U.S. Constitution*

suspend the students and that the school could not forbid students from expressing their political opinions unless the school could show that allowing the students to do this would "materially and substantially interfere with the requirements of appropriate discipline in the operation of the school." (*Tinker v. Des Moines School District*, 393 U.S. 503 (1969)) However, the judges said that their opinion did not necessarily apply to any disruptive behavior or even to group demonstrations.  The *Tinker* case applied to a specific set of circumstances and the decision of the court was by no means unanimous.  If you have a similar problem you should seek specific advice from a lawyer.

## PHYSICAL PUNISHMENT

*Can a teacher hit me or physically punish me?*

Yes.  A teacher or principal may use "reasonable force" to "restrain or correct" a student. (Minn. Stat. §609.06)  Naturally, this does not mean that he or she can really injure you.  A teacher who intentionally used more than reasonable force might be guilty of assault, a misdemeanor in Minnesota. (Minn. Stat. §609.22)  The U.S. Supreme Court has said that the use of corporal punishment does not violate the constitutional rights of the student. (*Ingraham v. Wright*, 430 U.S. 651 (1977))

## PRIVACY IN THE SCHOOL

*Can the principal open my locker without my permission?*



At present this is a confused area of the law.  There are conflicting rights involved in this question.  First, the principal of any school has an obligation to protect the health and welfare of the students.  In the past, the principal and teacher have stood in place of the parents (in loco parentis).  However, the Fourth Amendment to the Constitution forbids unreasonable searches and seizures.  There have been two ways in which courts have approached the question.  One is by application of the criminal law, the other is by application of an administrative concept.

When applying the criminal law, courts have viewed the Fourth and Fifth Amendments of the Constitution as barring any expulsions or suspensions of students based on evidence obtained by an unreasonable search or compelled self-incrimination.  The U.S. Supreme Court has said that searches conducted outside the judicial process (without prior approval by a judge or magistrate—without a warrant) are per se unreasonable. (*Coolidge v. New Hampshire*, 403 U.S. 43 (1971))  Then by applying the *Tinker* case, which says that a student does not lose constitutional rights when entering the schoolhouse gates, some courts have felt that a principal may not look in the locker of a student without the student's permission or a

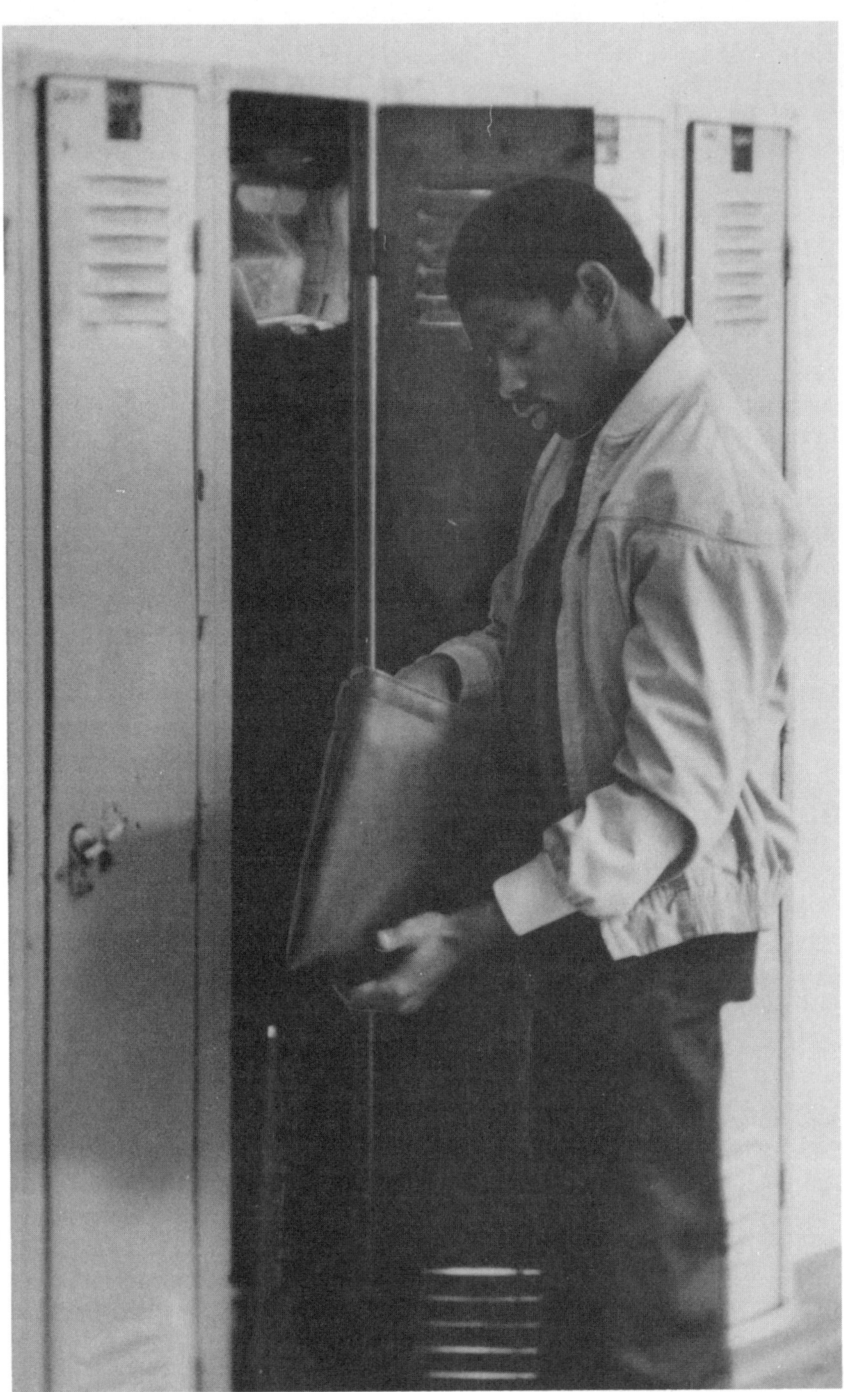

*Should a school administrator be allowed to search your locker?*

warrant. If any incriminating evidence is found in the locker, it may not be used against the student in a court of law, or for a suspension or expulsion.

However, some courts have applied the administrative concept. They view the opening of the locker by the principal as a valid exercise of authority, both as the administrator of the school—which is the true owner of the locker—and as a person who stands in place of the parents. These courts have felt that the primary purpose of the school official's search of a locker is not to obtain conviction of the student but rather to protect the student, and all the other students at the school. In the case of *People v. Overton* (20 N.Y.2d 360, 299 N.E.2d 596 (1967)), a New York court felt that even though the principal opened the locker without the permission of the student, the marijuana he found and turned over to the police was admissible in a criminal hearing against the student, since the principal was exercising an administrative function. One court in Kansas (*State v. Stein*, 203 Kan. 638, 456 P.2d 1 (1969)) stated: "We believe this right of inspection is inherent in the authority vested in school administrators and that the same must be retained and exercised in the management of our schools if their educational functions are to be maintained and the welfare of the student bodies preserved." The area of student locker searches and personal searches in the school is still unclear. Neither the Minnesota Supreme Court nor the U.S. Supreme Court has specifically addressed itself to this problem. There is also no specific state statute in the area.

CRIMINAL VIEW

Fourth Amendment + Tinker Case + Coolidge Case = No

ADMINISTRATIVE VIEW

Inherent authority of school principal + Overton Case + Stein Case = Yes

*Can my parents see my school records?*

Yes. There is a Minnesota law (Minn. Stat. §§15.1611 and 15.1698, entitled the Minnesota Government Data Practices Act, also known as Minnesota Data Privacy Act) and a federal law (20 U.S.C. §1232 et. seq., entitled the Family Educational Rights and Privacy Act of 1974, also known as the Buckley Amendment) which deal with this problem. The federal law permits the parents of students the right to inspect and review any and all official records, files, and data directly related to their children, including all material that is incorporated into that student's cumulative record folder, such as academic works completed, level of achievement (grades, standardized achievement tests, scores), attendance data, scores on standardized intelligence, aptitude, and psychological tests, interest inventory results, health data, family background information, teacher or counselor ratings and observations, and verified reports of serious or recurrent behavior patterns. The federal law also says that when a student reaches eighteen years of age, then only the student shall have the right to review the records.

*Can I look at my school records even though I am not yet eighteen years old?*

Minnesota law says that an individual who is the subject of the private data shall be shown that data upon request. (Minn. Stat.§15.165 subd. 3) The only data not available is certain confidential data defined by the law and certain private data such as financial records and statements of the student's parents. (Minn. Stat. 15.1693 subd. 3) Therefore, it seems that the Minnesota law allows students under eighteen to view the school records. However, there has been some dispute about the interpretation of the law in light of the federal law. Some have argued that the Minnesota law could not permit elementary children to see their records. So far this question remains unanswered.

*Who else besides my parents and me may look at my school records?*

Minnesota says that educational data on individuals is private and shall not be disclosed except to parents, certain authorized personnel (such as teachers, substitute teachers, and those governmental officials specifically authorized, such as commissioner of Education), or at certain times when it is necessary to disclose information in health and safety emergencies or with the consent of the parents or student. It has not been finally determined whether a police agent may review the school records of a student under the health and safety emergency exception of the law. (Minn. Stat. §15.1693 subd. 2)

*Can a teacher or the principal intercept and open a sealed note addressed to me?*

No. It is a misdemeanor to open intentionally any sealed letter, telegram, or package addressed to another without the permission of the addressee or the sender. (Minn. Stat. §609.795) This appears to apply to any sealed communication, whether transferred through public or private means.

## RELIGION IN THE SCHOOL

*May the public school start each day with a prayer?*

No. The First Amendment to the U.S. Constitution says, "Congress shall make no law respecting an *establishment* of religion, or prohibiting the *free exercise* thereof. . . ." In interpreting the meaning of the First Amendment Establishment Clause, the U.S. Supreme Court has decided a number of cases saying: (1) classes in religious instruction in public schools are not permissible (*McCollum v. Board of Education,* 333 U.S. 203 (1945)); (2) public schools may not start out each day with a prayer being said aloud (*Engel v. Vitale,* 370 U.S. 421 (1962)); and (3) public schools may not require that each day begin with a reading of ten verses of the Bible, nor read without comment the Lord's Prayer (*Abington v. Schempp,* 374 U.S. 203 (1963)). Even if the prayer readings are voluntary and the student can be excused, such readings are not permissible. The premise is that "a wall between church and state . . . must be kept high and impregnable." (Justice Hugo L. Black in his dissenting opinion in *Zorach v. Clauson,* 343 U.S. 306 (1952))

*Can I be released from school to attend religious services or instruction at my church?*

Yes. The law allows release time to take religious training up to three hours a week. (Minn. Stat. §120.10(c)) The U.S. Supreme Court has upheld laws permitting release time. (*Zorach v. Clauson*, 343 U.S. 306 (1952)) As long as the instruction is not at the public school, then the establishment clause is not violated.

*Is there a contradiction between the establishment clause and the free exercise clause?*

Some argue that by not permitting prayer in school the free exercise rights are violated. Others say by permitting such prayer the establishment clause is violated. The problems in this area show that the courts must constantly strive to balance the constitutional rights of the parties in conflict. The U.S. Supreme Court has said, "We are a religious people whose institutions presuppose a supreme being. We guarantee the freedom to worship as one chooses. We make room for as wide a variety of beliefs and creeds as the spirtual needs of man deem necessary. . . . [But] the government must be neutral when it comes to competition between sects. It may not thrust any sect on any person." (*Zorach v. Clauson*, 343 U.S. 306 (1952))

*Can we learn about the Bible and about religion and religious sects in the public school?*

Yes, it is permissible to learn about religion as long as there is no indoctrination in the particular religion being studied.

## HANDICAPPED STUDENTS

*Do handicapped students have a right to an education?*

Yes. In fact, the main thrust of Minnesota's law is that the handicapped student be "mainstreamed" into the regular classroom. To the maximum extent appropriate, handicapped children, including those in public or private institutions, are to be educated with children who are not handicapped. (Minn. Stat. §120.03) If mainstreaming is not appropriate, then the student has a right to be provided special classes by the school district. If the school district cannot provide the classes, then the parents can seek out private special schooling that is appropriate and require the school district to pay.

The federal law (the Education of All Handicapped Children Act (PL 91-230) amended through 1975 (PL 94-142)) requires that all handicapped children are given the right to a free appropriate education. Each handicapped student is entitled to an individual educational program (I.E.P.) to meet his or her needs, and if the public school cannot meet the needs, then free transportation and educational services must be provided by the school district in an appropriate setting.

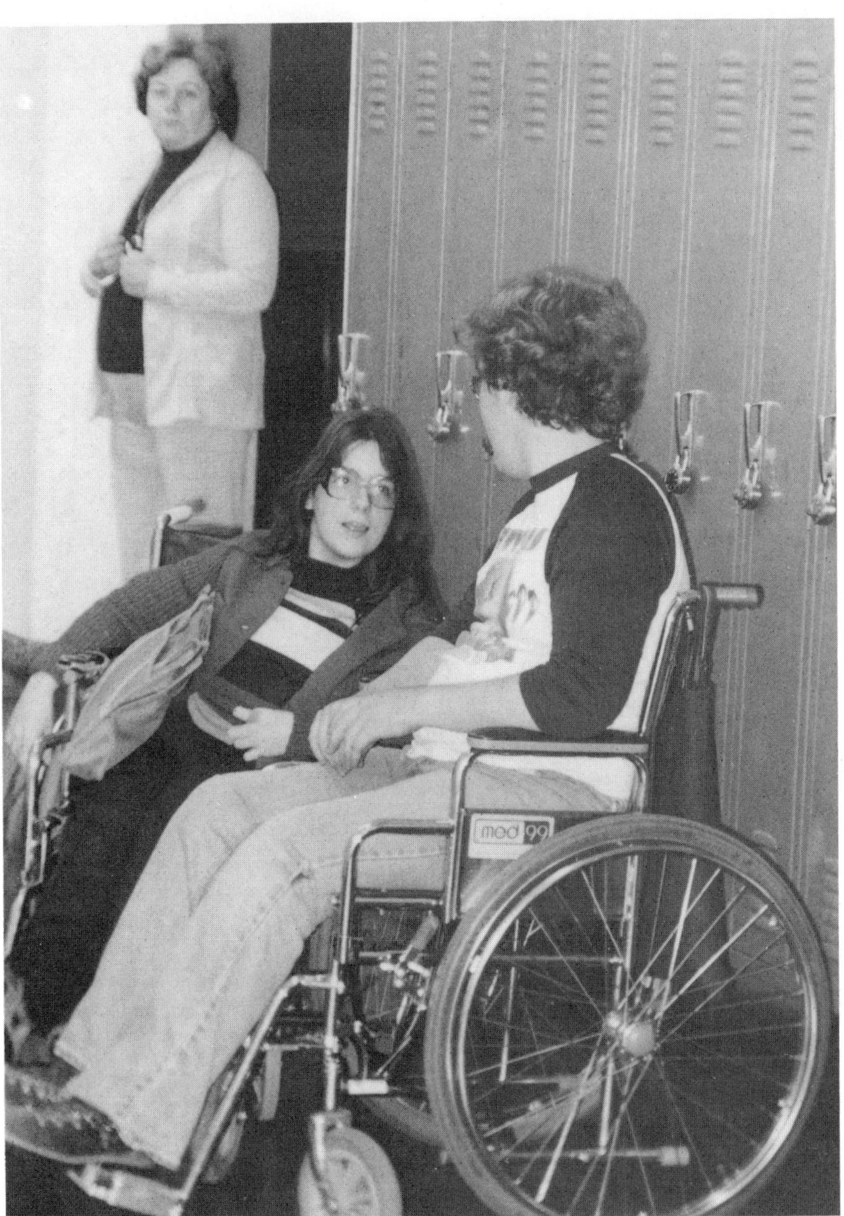

*The law requires schools to mainstream handicapped students.*

Both the Minnesota law and the federal law involve due process components (see Appendix B) if the parents object to the classification of the child or to the individualized educational program of the child. The due process involves a conciliation conference, a local hearing, a hearing before the commissioner of education (with a possible hearing before the State Hearing Examiner Office), and an appeal to the district court.

*Who is a handicapped student?*

The term *handicapped children* is defined to include children who have one or more of the following handicaps: (1) deafness or hard-of-hearing; (2) blindness or partial sight; (3) crippled condition (including pregnancy); (4) speech defect; (5) physical impairment; (6) educable or trainable mental retardation; (7) emotional disturbance; (8) learning disability; (9) special behavior problem. (Minn. Stat. §120.03)

## RIGHT TO AN EDUCATION

*Must the public schools allow me to attend?*

In general all persons over five and under twenty-one have a right to a free public school education. (Minn. Stat. §120.06)

*If I graduate from high school but cannot read, can I sue my teachers and school administrators?*

In 1972, a unique complaint of educational malpractice was filed by a young man in California. The case (*Peter W. v. San Francisco Unified School District*, 131 Cal. Rptr. 854 (1976)) was eventually dismissed by the California Court of Appeals but nevertheless has been viewed with interest by many state courts. So far, no student has been successful in such a lawsuit. (See also *Hoffman v. Board of Education*, 242 N.Y. Supp. 2d 376, which said for "policy reasons" the student could not recover damages.)

*If I am married can I be excluded from school?*

No. (Op. Atty. Gen., 169-i May 1, 1965).

*If I am pregnant can I be excluded from school?*

No. In fact, under the Minnesota handicapped law (Minn. Stat. §120.03) pregnancy is viewed as a handicap that requires the school to provide appropriate education.



## EQUALITY IN SCHOOL

*What kind of equality is being sought in school?*

The courts are requiring schools to provide equal educational opportunity in schools.

### Race

*Can a public school have separate but equal schools for the different races?*

No. In 1954 the U.S. Supreme Court said, "We conclude that in the field of public education the doctrine of "separate but equal" has no place. Separate educational facilities are inherently unequal." (*Brown v. Board of Education,* 347 U.S. 483)

*What do the terms* de jure *and* de facto mean?

*De jure* means "by law;" *de facto* means "by fact." In the race and education cases the courts have said that *de jure* segregation violates the fourteenth Amendment equal protection clause (see Appendix B), but *de facto* segregation does not. (*Keyes v. Denver School District #1,* 413 U.S. 921 (1973))

*Is busing a permissible tool to end de jure racial segregation in the public schools?*

Yes. Site selections, racial quotas, altering attendance zones, and transportation of students are all permissible tools to end *de jure* racial segregation in the public schools (*Swann v. Charlotte-Mecklenburg Board of Education,* 402 U.S. 1 (1971))

## Sex

*Can girls be excluded from playing varsity contact sports with boys?*

Yes. Title IX of the Educational Amendments of 1972 (20 U.S.C. §1681 et. seq.) prohibits any educational program receiving federal assistance from discriminating on the basis of sex. However, regulations published by the Department of Health, Education, and Welfare (HEW) in 1975 that enforces Title IX specifically authorizes separate sex teams where "selection for such teams is based upon competitive skill or the activity involved is a contact sport." (45 C.F.R. §86.41(b)) However, the regulation goes on to say that where a team sport (1) is operated for one sex only, (2) doesn't have a team for the opposite sex, and (3) limits the athletic opportunities for members of that sex, then members of the excluded sex must be allowed to try out for the team offered unless the sport involved is a contact sport. So in one case (*Gomes v. Rhode Island Interscholastic League,* 469 F. Supp. 659 (1979)) a high school boy was permitted to try out for the girls' volleyball team because there was no boys' volleyball team. Minnesota had a case that permitted girls to try out for the boys' high school tennis and cross-country running and skiing teams where there were no female teams. (*Brenden v. Independent School District 742,* 477 F. 2d 1292 (8th Cir. 1973))

In 1975, the legislature passed a law mandating that educational institutions and public services make every reasonable effort to provide substantially equal athletic budgets for both sexes. (Minn. Stat. 126.21(3)) The law further specifies that it is not unfairly discriminatory "to restrict membership on an athletic team to participants of one sex, if this restriction is necessary to provide members of each sex with an equal opportunity to participate in the athletic program" or "to provide two teams in the same sport which are in fact separated or substantially separated according to sex, if the two teams are provided with substantially equal budgets per participant." (Minn. Stat. §§126.21(1) and (2))

Some national cases of interest include those in which a ten-year-old girl was allowed in little league baseball (*Forten v. Darlington Little League, Inc.*, 514 F. 2d 344 (1st Cir. 1975)), and physically qualified girls were *permitted* to play varsity basketball (*Yellow Spring School District v. Ohio High School Athletic Association*, 443 F. Supp. 753 (1978)). But compare these cases with cases that said it was permissible to exclude females from high school basketball even where there was no team for females (*Carros v. Tennessee Secondary School Athletic Association*, 415 F. Supp. 569 (1976); a high school soccer team can be limited to males (*Hoover v. Meiklejohn*, 430 F. Supp. 164 (D. Colo. 1977)); a twelve-year-old girl was excluded from football in a recreational league (*Clinton v. Nogy*, 411 F. Supp. 1396 (N.D. Ohio 1974)). Obviously, there continues to be disagreement over the meaning and interpretation of the law.

## Bilingual Education

*Must non-English-speaking students receive their education in their native tongue?*

The law is very confusing on this issue. The U.S. Supreme Court has ruled that teaching non-English-speaking Chinese students without giving them special English courses or without giving instructions in Chinese violates Title VI of the Civil Rights of 1964. (*Lau v. Nichols*, 414 U.S. 563 (1974)) In 1970 HEW issued guidelines that said, "Where inability to speak and understand the English language excludes national origin-minority group children from effective participation in the educational program offered by a school district, the district must take affirmative steps to rectify the language deficiency in order to open its instructional program to these students." (35 Fed. Reg. 11595)

The problem today is that there seems to be two distinctly different purposes behind bilingual education programs: (1) assimilating the minority into the dominate culture, and (2) maintaining and enriching the minority culture. If the assimilation purpose is the main motivation, then the method used to educate the non-English-speaking student should be special English classes with mainstreaming in all other classes. If the purpose is to maintain the culture, then instruction in all the courses in the native tongue would be the method.

At this time the debate continues as to which is the better way to achieve the Supreme Court's directive that the non-English-speaking students receive equal educational opportunity.

## Financing Education

*Must my school spend equal amounts of money for each student?*

No. The schools must attempt to provide equal educational opportunity, but to do this it may require different amounts of money to be spent per student.

For example, it may cost more to provide a handicapped student with equal educational opportunity. (See *San Antonio Independent School District v. Rodriques*, 409 U.S. 822 (1973))


## SEX EDUCATION

*Can my school have a sex education program if I and my parents object?*

Yes. The Minnesota Constitution requires a general and uniform system of public schools. (Minnesota Constitution Article 8, §§1-3) In designing such a system the legislature has given power to the Minnesota Board of Education to design a general curriculum. Sex education can be part of that curriculum. The Board of Education is granted broad discretionary power in formulating and enacting educational programs for the state's public schools. (*Associated Schools of Independent District #63 of Hector, Renville County v. School District #83 of Renville County*, 122 Minn. 254 (1913)) Some have argued that their privacy and religious rights are violated by sex education. Generally the courts have said that it is permissible for schools to offer sex education courses such as "Human Sexuality" and "Family Life" but that individual exemption from such courses must also be permitted. (*Valent v. New Jersey State Board of Education*, 274 A 2d 832 (1971); *Medleros v. Kiyosaki*, 52 Hawaii 436 (1970); *Citizens for Parental Rights v. San Mateo County Board of Education*, 124 Cal. Rptr. 68 (1975))


## SMOKING IN SCHOOL

*If I'm over eighteen can I smoke in school?*

This is a very difficult problem for students and school officials. If you are under eighteen it is illegal to smoke. (Minn. Stat. §609.685; see also Chapter 8.) In Minnesota the Clean Indoor Air Act (Minn. Stat. §§144.411-144.417) provides that no person shall smoke in a public place or at a public meeting. The local school boards have authority to make rules and regulations for orderly government of schools. (Minn. Stat. §123.33 subd. 7) Therefore the school board has the authority to forbid all smoking by students over eighteen or, if it wishes, to provide a lounge area designated a smoking area for students over eighteen. Most schools have chosen to ban all smoking except in designated areas, but to provide a designated smoking area only for teachers.


## PROBLEM 1

Tom, Dick, and Harriet, three students at East-Southeast High School, decided that the school paper does not speak for the majority of students; they decided to put out an underground newspaper that would really fulfill that function. Their first issue was produced on stencils that Tom stole from the school office. The issue was run on the school mimeograph machine without permission.

The paper contained the following: a column making some untrue statements about the principal's sex life; a list of "ratings" of the various teachers, mostly in obscene and abusive language; a "letter to the editor" written by Harriet in which she criticized the school's grading system, called for the resignation of the assistant principal on grounds of incompetence, and urged all students to stay out of school on a particular day as a protest against the bad food served in the cafeteria.

After the paper had been mimeographed, Dick, who had no part in writing the material, distributed the paper to every student he could find by standing in front of the cafeteria door, disrupting traffic, and making many students late for class. The teachers complained that their students read the paper in class and didn't pay attention to the class work because of their interest in the scandalous and controversial material in the paper.

The school administration, upon discovering who was responsible for the paper, summarily dismissed Tom, Dick, and Harriet from school by means of a short letter saying merely that, because of conduct unbecoming a student, they were permanently expelled and would not be eligible for readmission.

1. Has any of the three students committed a crime?

2. Has any of them committed a tort?

3. Has the school the right to dismiss them? Why or why not?

4. Could the school forbid them from publishing their newspaper? From distributing it during school hours?

NOW!
SAVE $80
219 95

# 7

# CONSUMER LAW

You can help yourself and solve some of your problems if you know your rights and remedies.* This chapter will explain some of your basic rights involving sales practices, car sales, warranties, checks, credit, and collection. Many of these laws are based upon common sense, and your common sense and what appears to you to be a reasonable solution to a problem will oftentimes be your best remedy. You will need to speak up and complain to someone about your problem. This chapter will provide you with some information to increase your ability, knowledge, and confidence to help yourself.

*Portions of this chapter have been taken from the *Minnesota Consumer Law Handbook* with the permission of its author, Roger S. Haydock.

## CONTENTS

## CASE STUDY

STUDENT:   *The stereo equipment we bought on credit doesn't work and needs to be fixed.*

CREDITOR:   *We don't have to fix it. Didn't you read the warranty?*

STUDENT:   *That's not our understanding of the agreement. Unless you repair or replace the stereo, we won't pay.*

CREDITOR:   *Pay us or we'll sue you.*

STUDENT:   *We won't pay you for the goods, and we won't pay any interest charges.*

CREDITOR:   *If you don't pay us, we'll just take back the stereo and repossess some of your other property.*

1. What can you as a consumer do?

---

**SELF-QUIZ**

Before you read the chapter, try the following quiz. Answer each question as best you can, based on your general knowledge. When you have read the chapter, go back to see whether or not you have changed your mind about any of the answers.

1. A seller can tell a consumer one thing before a sale and then change his or her mind after the sale and tell that consumer another thing. _______ True _______ False

2. If a consumer receives something in the mail that was not requested, the consumer must send it back. _______ True _______ False

3. A consumer who buys something in the home from a door-to-door salesperson can cancel that sale for any reason within three days after the sale. _______ True _______ False

4. Every time a consumer buys something, he or she receives a warranty that covers that good or product. _______ True _______ False

5. It is permissible for a salesperson to give opinions and use "puffing" to sell a product. _______ True _______ False

6. Common remedies available to a consumer for a breach of a warranty include demanding that the goods be repaired or replaced or that the consumer be refunded his or her money. _______ True _______ False

7. If someone steals a consumer's checks and forges a signature and cashes them, the consumer will be responsible for paying the bank for such checks. _______ True _______ False

8. Credit arises when a consumer buys some goods or services or receives a loan and agrees to pay later. _______ True _______ False

9. Interest is the same thing as a finance charge. _______ True _______ False

10. A consumer always has to pay a credit card bill even though the goods bought with the card are defective. _______ True _______ False

11. If a consumer is denied credit, the creditor does not have to tell the consumer why credit was denied. _______ True _______ False

12. A collection agency can call late at night and early in the morning to try and collect a debt from a consumer.  _______ True _______ False
13. A creditor can break into a consumer's home and take the consumer's property if the consumer does not pay for it.  _______ True _______ False
14. There is not much consumers can do to solve their own problems. _______ True _______ False

## DECEPTIVE SALES PRACTICES

*What is a deceptive sales practice?*

Any advertisement, statement, or conduct by a seller of goods or services that deceives, misleads, or confuses you is a deceptive practice and a violation of the law.

*What is a good?*

A good is any product or item that you buy, like a car, stereo, or clothes.

*What is a service?*

A service is something a seller does for you, like providing repair services, or racquetball facilities, or dance lessons.

*What are some examples of deceptive sales approaches?*

A seller may advertise some product for sale but not intend actually to sell it. A seller may advertise an item for sale at a low price and then, after you come to the store, tell you that the item is no good and attempt to sell you a more expensive or more profitable item. This practice is called "bait and switch." The seller "baits" you to come to the store and then "switches" you to another product.

Sellers may advertise a sale and not have a reasonable supply of the product in the store. The law prohibits the seller from such advertisement unless the seller either advertises the limited number of such items or provides you with a "raincheck" that allows you to return and buy the item at the sale price at a later date. You can also accept substitute products if available.

A seller of services may tell you that certain services will be provided at certain prices and later not provide those services at those prices. They will then claim you must have misunderstood something or claim that the contract you signed does not provide those services.

Other examples include:

■ Sellers who have consumers sign blank contracts and later fill in the contract terms.

■ Sellers who "guarantee" their product "100%" only to refuse to honor that warranty later.

■ Sellers who tell customers one thing before a sale and then later deny saying that, or change their minds and tell the consumer something else.

*What remedies does the law provide the consumer who is involved in a deceptive practice?*

The law permits the consumer to sue the seller and recover money damages and have the seller pay for attorney's fees if the consumer is successful.

## Unsolicited Goods

*What happens if some seller sends me something in the mail that I did not request? What can I do?*

You can do whatever you want with what you receive. (Minn. Stat. §325.92) This unsolicited good is a gift and you, the recipient, may keep or dispose of the item in any way you want. You have no obligation to pay for the item or even send it back.

## Sales Disclosure

*How do I know someone is trying to sell me something?*

This question arises in sales approaches made outside a store. The law requires a seller to disclose to you certain information before attempting a sale. (Minn. Stat. §325.943) Any time a seller contacts you by telephone or at your home, that seller must provide you before making any sales presentation with:

■ His or her name,

■ The name of the business or company,

■ An identification card (in door-to-door sales),

■ A description of the kind of goods or services for sale,

■ An explanation about what the seller wants to do (usually some demonstration or explanation of the good or service).

*Does every seller have to explain all this?*

No. The law excludes nonprofit organizations, like scouts, school fund raisers, and church groups.

## Door-to-Door Sales

*Does a consumer receive any protection from door-to-door sales?*

Both federal and Minnesota law permit you to change your mind and cancel a door-to-door sales contract. These sales include purchases that amount to more than twenty-five dollars that you make in your home and not at a merchant's store. You have three business days (excluding Saturdays, Sundays, and holidays) after agreeing to such a sale or after receiving the notice to cancel that purchase. You do not need any reason to cancel; you can simply change your mind. Your cancellation notice must be in writing, either mailed or delivered to the merchant within three business days of the sale.

*Do I receive any notice of this "cooling-off" period at the time of the sale?*

Yes. The seller must provide you with a copy of the "notice of cancellation," which explains your right to cancel and details what you have to do to cancel the contract.

## Used Car Mileage

*I'm going to buy a used car. How do I know the mileage reading is accurate?*

The law requires that the seller must disclose in writing the true mileage on the odometer, or, if the true mileage is unknown, that information must also be disclosed. (Minn. Stat. §325.823)

*What if a person tampers with the odometer?*

No person shall knowingly tamper with, adjust, alter, set back, or disconnect an odometer to cause a lower mileage reading than has actually been driven. If a person does that, he or she is guilty of a gross misdemeanor. (Minn. Stat. §325.822)

*How does the law help me?*

You can recover up to three times the actual damages or $1,500, whichever is greater. This can include a reasonable attorney's fee. (Minn. Stat. §325.824)

## WARRANTIES

*When I buy a product do I get any protection?*

Generally when you buy a good, the seller is required to make certain promises or warranties about the item you have just purchased. But not every sale includes a warranty.

**WHAT DO YOU THINK?**

Donna recently moved into her new apartment when a door-to-door pots and pans salesman talked her into signing a contract for $750 worth of goods. Now she is having second thoughts about this. What can she do? Does any person need this amount of cookware? What possible pressure tactics might have been used on Donna? How do door-to-door salespeople gain entry into homes and apartments? What can you do and how should you respond to high-pressure sales tactics? How do high-pressure salespeople try to make you feel?

*A car may be one of your first major purchases.*

*What is a warranty?*

A warranty is a guarantee about the quality and condition of the good.

*Are there different types of warranties?*

Yes.  There are express warranties and implied warranties.

## Express Warranties

*What is an express warranty?*

An express warranty is something a seller writes, says, or does that is an affirmation of fact about the goods.  The seller may be either a merchant or another consumer selling something.

*What are the different ways express warranties can be created?*

An express warranty can be created by the seller providing you with a written warranty, by telling you certain facts about the product during a sales talk, by advertising the goods in newspapers, over television, on radio, by displaying a sample of the product, or in some other way promoting the product.

*Is there always a written warranty when I buy something?*

If you buy something new, you usually will receive a written warranty with that product.  If you buy something used, you may or may not receive a written warranty from the seller.  A Federal Warranty Law requires that all written warranties contain the following information:

1.  A description of the parts covered by the warranty and the parts not covered.

2.  A statement of what the warrantor (the person or company making the warranty) will do under the warranty.  This provision may include a statement that the goods will be repaired or replaced, or a statement describing the parts or labor that the warrantor will pay for, or some other similar statement.

3.  How long the warranty will be effective.

4.  The name of the warrantor.

5.  The mailing address of the warrantor or a free telephone number.

6.  An explanation of the steps that you must follow to get satisfaction under the warranty.

7.  The statement, "This warranty gives you specific legal rights and you may also have other rights which vary from state to state."

8.  Exactly whom the warranty covers if it doesn't apply to everyone.

9.  When the warranty begins (if that time is different from the date of your purchase).

10.  Limitations on implied warranties (warranties added to sales contracts by the law), which must be disclosed prominently in large or noticeable type on the front of the warranty and must include the statement, "Some states do not allow limitations on how long an implied warranty lasts, so the above limitations may not apply to you."  Minnesota law doesn't allow sellers to limit the time on express written warranties for new goods, but does allow them to limit the time on used goods or on sales that include no express written warranty.

11.  Any restrictions on damages you may recover, which must be shown prominently in large or noticeable type on the front of the warranty and must include the statement, "Some states do not allow the exclusion or the limitation of incidental or consequential damages, so the above limitations may not apply to you."  Minnesota law allows limitation on these types of damages, depending on the facts of the case.  Incidental damages are those

damages directly related to the goods becoming defective, such as the cost of towing a broken-down car and the cost of repairs caused by a defective car. Consequential damages include other related losses resulting from the defective product, such as loss of income from a job because of a car breaking down on the way to work. To avoid having to pay for such incidental and consequential damages, a seller has to tell you about the limitations, using the exact format and language of this section.

**12.** The effect of a registration card. Some sellers use a card (usually called a warranty registration card) that you must send to the seller for the warranty to take effect. The seller has to tell you what to do with such a card. If you don't mail in the card, you may have no warranty protection.

*Will there always be an express oral warranty when I buy something?*

That depends on what the salesperson tells you about the product. Not everything a salesperson tells you about a product becomes a warranty. Oral warranties are based on statements of fact. The law allows a salesperson to tell you his or her opinion and to use persuasive statements. A seller may use sales talk or "puffing" when speaking about a product. (Minn. Stat. §§336.2-313(2))

*How do I know what is an express oral warranty and what is an opinion?*

Buyers must use good judgment to separate warranties from opinions. These are examples of opinions:

1.  This is the finest water heater money can buy.

2.  This car is the best in its class.

These are examples of warranties:

1.  This water heater has a capacity of forty-nine gallons.

2.  This car has six cylinders.

## Implied Warranties

*What is an implied warranty?*

An implied warranty is a guarantee that comes with the product just because you bought it. The warranty arises even if the seller did not tell you about it or give you a written description of it.

An example of an implied warranty is called the warranty of merchantibility. Actually, it is a group of warranties that provides certain minimum standards the item you  purchased must meet. Sometimes this warranty has been called the warranty of fitness for ordinary purposes or fit for normal use. (Minn. Stat. §336.2-314) In other words, the goods must do what they are supposed to do.

*Does the warranty of merchantibility cover every sale?*

No. It covers only a sale by a merchant, a person who deals in goods of the kind or who has knowledge or skill about the product. This warranty would not arise if you bought a car from a friend. (Minn. Stat. §336.2-104)

*Are there other implied warranties?*

Yes. Another warranty is called the warranty of fitness for a particular purpose. This may occur any time you buy something from any seller, not just a merchant. When you tell the seller you will be using the item for a certain purpose and he or she helps you pick out the proper item and you depend on what you are told, then the seller has made an implied warranty that the goods shall be fit for such purpose. (Minn. Stat. §336.2-315)

*Do I always get these warranties when I buy something?*

No. The seller may modify or disclaim the warranty.

*How may a seller disclaim or modify the warranty?*

A seller or manufacturer may tell you prior to your purchase or in a writing by using large, noticeable words that the sale is "as is" or "with all faults" and the entire risk as to the quality and performance of the goods is with the buyer. (Minn. Stat. §336.2-316(3) and Minn. Stat. §325.952 sub. 2)

## Service Contract

*What is a service contract?*

Sellers may provide a contract in addition to or instead of a warranty. This contract may cover service work for parts and labor to repair a product. For example, a seller may provide a one-year written warranty and offer to sell you for fifty dollars a service contract that will cover the cost of repairs for a second year. This service contract is like an insurance policy. If anything goes wrong with the product during the second year, this contract will pay for the repairs.

## Remedies

*What can I do if what I bought does not work?*

You can first contact the seller and request that something be done to remedy your problem. Many sellers will help you and solve your problem without you having to complain forcefully. Some stores will give you another item, or a substitute product, or your money back. They may do this to honor your warranties or may do so to maintain good customer relations. If a seller does not do what you request, then you may have to demand your rights under warranty law.

**WHAT DO YOU THINK?**

Olga purchased a stereo from Retail Stereo store. It had a 100% express warranty for 90 days. Retail Stereo stores offered a service contract for $50 per year, increasing by $5 each year. The stereo cost $500. Should Olga buy the service contract? What factors should she weigh in deciding?

*How do I go about demanding my rights?*

You first have to claim that there is a warranty covering the product. If there is a written warranty, that will be the basis of your rights. If there was an express oral warranty made by the salesperson, that statement will be the basis for your rights. If there has been no "disclaimer" or avoiding by the seller of the implied warranties, the implied warranties will be the basis of your rights. Usually there will be more than one of these three types of warranties in a situation.

*What do I do after I establish a warranty?*

You need to notify the seller and complain about the product not working and ask that something be done about it. The law requires you to notify the seller when a product doesn't work. The law further gives the seller a right to try to fix the product if the seller wants to. You can notify the seller by telephone, by letter, or in person.

*What if the seller still does not want to do what I want done?*

You can again try to discuss matters with the seller and attempt to reach some compromise, or you can demand certain remedies in certain situations. You may have one or more of three alternatives:

1. You may request that the product be repaired or replaced.

2. You may be able to return the goods and demand your money back.

3. You may keep the goods and deduct the repair costs or ask for reimbursement for any repair costs.

What you do depends upon a number of things. Two common factors are the kind of warranty you have and the nature of the repairs required.

*What if there is a written warranty?*

If there is a written warranty, the remedy that you will have available will be explained in that warranty. The seller or manufacturer will usually limit which of the three basic remedies you will have. Usually you will be limited to having the goods either repaired or replaced at the option of the seller— that is, whichever is the more reasonable option. The law requires the seller to follow the terms of the written warranty and may require the seller to go beyond those terms if the remedies provided do not adequately provide you with an appropriate remedy.

*What about the kind of repairs required if there is no written warranty?*

If a product has major defects that require substantial repairs, or if the repairs will take a long time, or if the repairs will cost more than the price of the goods, you can usually demand that the product be replaced and not repaired.

If a product has minor defects that require small repairs, or if the repairs can be completed within a reasonable time, or if the repairs are not expensive compared to the cost of the goods, then you will usually be entitled to have the goods repaired and not replaced.

*When can I demand a refund of my money and return the goods?*

You can demand a refund of your money or refuse to pay if the seller refuses to honor the warranty, or if the seller refuses to repair or replace the defective product unless the written warranty provides a different remedy, or if the goods remain defective after the seller unsuccessfully tries to repair them, or if the replacement goods become defective. You cannot demand that the merchant take back the goods for any defect. The defect must be a major one and not a minor flaw.

*When can I keep the goods and either deduct or demand reimbursement for repair costs?*

You can keep the defective goods, have them repaired, and deduct the cost of repairs from what you owe the merchant or demand that the merchant reimburse you for the repair cost. You may want to do this in situations where the defects are minor and not major and you want to keep the goods. The law permits you to do so and to recover your repair costs if the seller refuses to repair the goods. You can then have someone else do the repairs and require the seller either to reimburse you or to deduct the repair cost from the credit balance you may owe the seller.

*This sounds somewhat confusing. What else can be done?*

Some sellers will solve your problem merely by your asking for a reasonable solution. Other sellers will not help you. You need to know and understand your rights and remedies so that you can assert your warranty rights.

## CHECKS

*What is a check?*

A check is a written order directed to the consumer's bank to pay a certain sum of money to the order of the party named on the check. You first must establish a checking account with a bank and deposit money in that account to obtain checks.

*Why use checks?*

Checks may be more convenient to use than money. Checks may be safer than money which, when lost, cannot be replaced. And checks when returned by the bank after having been "canceled" (paid) act as receipts.

*What happens if checks are stolen, altered, or forged?*

The bank is authorized to cash only checks that bear the consumer's signature.  Checks that are stolen and signed by someone who is not the consumer (forged) are not checks that the bank should pay. If the bank does pay these checks, it cannot take money from the consumer's account or demand that the consumer pay.  The bank is liable (it must pay). However, if a consumer is negligent (careless) in such a way that makes it easy for a wrongdoer to forge the signature or to change the amount of the check, the consumer could become liable for the check or for the altered amount.  For example, if you left your checkbook and your driver's license with a copy of your signature on it with a known forger, you might be liable for the forger's acts.  Similarly, if you sign a check but leave blanks where the amount is written so that someone might easily change the words and figures, you might be liable for the raised amount.

Each month your bank will send you a statement listing the checks that have been paid and the deposits that have been made and showing how much was in your account at the time the statement was prepared. The bank will also send you the canceled checks that it has paid.  The consumer must look at these checks and tell the bank if there are forgeries or alterations. This must be done as soon as possible.

*What is a "bad" check?*

A "bad" check is one that a consumer writes for an amount in excess of the balance in the checking account.  In other words, the consumer has an insufficient bank balance to cover the amount of the check.  The consumer can deposit money in that account before the check passes through the bank. Or a consumer may have a special checking account with the bank by which the bank will cover this "overdrawn" amount.  The consumer will then have to pay the bank for covering the amount of the check plus interest, because this transaction is like a loan of money, even though it may be only for a short time.

*How long does it take before the check a consumer gives a seller is processed by the consumer's bank?*

That primarily depends upon when the seller deposits the check with its bank.  Here is what happens:  the seller deposits your check in its bank and receives credit. This bank then transfers the check to a "clearinghouse" bank which, in turn, transfers the check to the consumer's bank.  The consumer's bank takes the amount of the check from the consumer's account and transfers that money to the seller's bank. This process may take only a day or as long as several days.

*Is it a crime for a consumer to write a bad check?*

That depends upon the circumstances.  If a consumer writes a check and knows there are insufficient funds in the account and intends not to add money to the account, then it is a crime.  Or if a consumer writes a check on an account that has been closed, this is also a crime.  The consumer has to write a worthless check intentionally or intend to defraud the seller for it to be a crime.

*What is a "bounced" check?*

A "bounced" check is one the bank refuses to pay.  Usually this will be because the consumer does not have enough money in the account, but it could happen for other reasons.  For example, a creditor might have **garnished** the bank account.

*What should you do if your check bounces?*

You should call the person you wrote the check to and advise him or her that you have or will put money in the account and ask them to "run" the check through again.  Then deposit the necessary money in your account.  If that person refuses to do so and there is no question that you owe the money, you should pay him or her in cash, but be sure that you get your check back.

*What is a postdated check?*

A postdated check is one the consumer writes on one day but dates with a later date, intending that the check not be cashed before that date.  For example, a consumer may give someone a check on January 1 and date the check January 5.  The check can then be cashed on January 5.  Consumers will postdate checks to pay for something at a later date or to give them time to deposit money in an account.  But most banks include in their agreements with their customers a provision that allows the bank to pay a check even before the date written on it.  You should not give a postdated check to someone unless you are sure that person will hold it until the date.

*When can a consumer stop payment on a check?*

A consumer can order a bank not to cover a check by simply telling the bank not to honor that check.  To be effective, this request has to be made before the bank processes the check.  You should do this only if you have good reason.  The oral **stop order** is only good for fourteen days.  If the check was presented to your bank after the fourteen days, the bank would pay it.  If you want to keep the stop order effective for a longer period, you can sign a written stop order form that will be effective for six months.  Banks make a charge, usually two dollars or three dollars, for stop orders.

*What is a certified check?*

A certified check is a check the consumer's bank promises to pay.  The bank has charged the consumer's account and will not stop payment on the check even if the consumer requests that it do so.

**garnishment:** a proceeding where a person's property, money, or credits in possession of another are applied to payment of the former's debt.

**stop order:** an oral or written statement by the writer of a check to his/her bank not to pay the check when it comes to the bank.

*What is a cashier's check?*

A cashier's check is a check issued by a bank that the bank draws on itself. An officer of the bank signs it. You can give a bank cash and it will issue a cashier's check for you. There is generally a charge for this service.

*Is a check cash?*

It is as good as cash if the seller accepts it. Most sellers will require the consumer to show some identification before accepting a check. Some sellers will not accept checks because they have lost too much money by accepting bad checks.

*What is the best way to avoid checking account problems?*

By balancing the account and making certain you do not write a check for an amount in excess of the balance. Banks also have special checking accounts that you may qualify for that will cover such checks.

## CREDIT

*What is credit?*

Credit arises whenever you delay payments for goods or services or money that you receive. Any time you use a credit card, sign an installment contract, or obtain a loan, you have used credit.

*What is interest?*

This is the charge you pay for the use of credit. Federal law requires creditors to provide you with a detailed disclosure form when you obtain credit. This form tells you the terms of the credit transaction. One of the terms is called the *finance charge*, which is the same thing as interest. This finance charge is listed both in a dollar amount and a percentage rate. This percentage is called the *annual percentage rate*.

*What is usury?*

The usury law sets a maximum rate of interest on credit transactions. The rate of interest a creditor may charge is regulated by a specific law that establishes the maximum rate for a specific type of credit transaction. These rates vary from six percent to thirty-six percent simple annual interest.

### Credit Transactions

*What are the most common forms of credit transactions?*

Installment contracts, loans, open end accounts, and mortgages.
Sellers (like car dealers) will sell you goods (like a car) on a retail

installment contract in which you agree to pay a cash price plus a finance charge for the goods over a period of time in installment payments (usually monthly).

Lenders (like banks, loan companies, and credit unions) lend you cash and in return you promise to pay the money back plus interest at a set amount each month over a period of time.

Both sellers and lenders allow you to buy things or to obtain a loan through open end credit accounts. These accounts include credit cards, special checking accounts, and machine cards. When you use a credit card to buy something in a store, when you write checks for an amount greater than the balance in a special account, when you use a card and punch special code numbers on a machine to obtain money, you have used an open end transaction. The creditor will send you a bill requiring you to pay the unpaid balance of your account plus interest if you do not pay within so many days. These accounts are called open end because you can obtain credit and pay for it in one or more payments over a period of time.

Financial institutions (savings and loan associations and banks) loan you money to buy a home. These transactions are called mortgages.

## Credit Terms

*What are the usual terms of a credit transaction and what do they mean?*

The exact terms of a credit transaction depend upon the type of transaction. Creditors usually use form agreements that detail the terms.

When you borrow money from a lender you will receive a copy of a disclosure statement, which lists the credit terms similar to the form shown in Figure 7-1. The following list defines these terms.

1. ANNUAL PERCENTAGE RATE—The interest rate over a year.

2. FINANCE CHARGE—The dollar amount of interest for the full term of the loan.

3. AMOUNT FINANCED—The amount of money you will have the actual use of; in other words, the amount of money you receive. The amount financed may also include some charges such as notary, investigation, or other fees.

4. TOTAL OF PAYMENTS—The full amount of what you must pay to the creditor, including all costs and charges.

5. NUMBER AND DATES OF PAYMENTS—These dates tell you when you must make your first payment, what day of the month future payments must be made, and the date of the last payment due.

6. AMOUNT OF PAYMENTS—This figure tells you the dollar amount of each installment.

7. FILING FEE—You may pay a fee for recording the loan agreement and papers with state or local officials.



Fill in Figure 7-1, Loan Model Form, based on this situation: Alfredo buys a 1978 Volkswagen from Jake's Used Cars for $2,000. He receives $300 as a trade in for his 1968 Plymouth. The recording fee is $6. His down payment is $500. The finance charge is 18% simple interest. He wishes to pay the amount owed in twenty-four months. How much will the car actually cost Alfredo?

*Managing your money is a big part of being a consumer.*

When you buy goods or services from a seller, the credit terms will be disclosed in the retail installment contract similar to the credit sale contract shown in Figure 7-2. These terms mean the same thing as the terms that appear in Figure 7-1. The one additional term—Total Sale Price—includes a subtotal of your down payment and the total of payments.

## FIGURE 7-1   Loan Model Form

| ANNUAL PERCENTAGE RATE<br><br>The cost of your credit as a yearly rate. | FINANCE CHARGE<br><br>The dollar amount the credit will cost you. | Amount Financed<br><br>The amount of credit provided to you or on your behalf. | Total of Payments<br><br>The amount you will have paid after you have made all payments as scheduled. |
|---|---|---|---|
| % | $ | $ | $ |

You have the right to receive at this time an itemization of the Amount Financed.
  ☐ I want an itemization.        ☐ I do not want an itemization.

Your payment schedule will be:

| Number of Payments | Amount of Payments | When Payments Are Due |
|---|---|---|
|  |  |  |
|  |  |  |

**Insurance**
Credit life insurance and credit disability insurance are not required to obtain credit, and will not be provided unless you sign and agree to pay the additional cost.

| Type | Premium | Signature |
|---|---|---|
| Credit Life |  | I want credit life insurance. _______________ Signature |
| Credit Disability |  | I want credit disability insurance. _______________ Signature |
| Credit Life and Disability |  | I want credit life and disability insurance. _______________ Signature |

You may obtain property insurance from anyone you want that is acceptable to        (creditor).        If you get the insurance

from        (creditor),        you will pay $______________ .

**Security:**  You are giving a security interest in:
  ☐    the goods or property being purchased.
  ☐    (brief description of other property).

**Filing fees** $ ______________          **Non-filing insurance** $ ______________

**Late Charge:** If a payment is late, you will be charged $ ______________ / ______________ % of the payment.

**Prepayment:** If you pay off early, you
  ☐ may    ☐ will not    have to pay a penalty.
  ☐ may    ☐ will not    be entitled to a refund of part of the finance charge.

See your contract documents for any additional information about nonpayment, default, any required repayment in full before the scheduled date, and prepayment refunds and penalties.

______________
e means an estimate

**FIGURE 7-2   Credit Sale Model Form**

| ANNUAL PERCENTAGE RATE<br>The cost of your credit as a yearly rate. | FINANCE CHARGE<br>The dollar amount the credit will cost you. | Amount Financed<br>The amount of credit provided to you or on your behalf. | Total of Payments<br>The amount you will have paid after you have made all payments as scheduled. | Total Sale Price<br>The total cost of your purchase on credit, including your downpayment of<br>$ ______________ |
|---|---|---|---|---|
| % | $ | $ | $ | $ |

You have the right to receive at this time an itemization of the Amount Financed.
☐ I want an itemization.      ☐ I do not want an itemization.

Your payment schedule will be:

| Number of Payments | Amount of Payments | When Payments Are Due |
|---|---|---|
|  |  |  |
|  |  |  |

**Insurance**
Credit life insurance and credit disability insurance are not required to obtain credit, and will not be provided unless you sign and agree to pay the additional cost.

| Type | Premium | Signature |
|---|---|---|
| Credit Life |  | I want credit life insurance. _______ Signature |
| Credit Disability |  | I want credit disability insurance. _______ Signature |
| Credit Life and Disability |  | I want credit life and disability insurance. _______ Signature |

You may obtain property insurance from anyone you want that is acceptable to (creditor). If you get the insurance from (creditor), you will pay $______________.

**Security:** You are giving a security interest in:
☐ the goods or property being purchased.
☐ (brief description of other property).

**Filing fees $** ____________          **Non-filing insurance $** ____________

**Late Charge:** If a payment is late, you will be charged $ ____________ / ____________ % of the payment.

**Prepayment:** If you pay off early, you
☐ may   ☐ will not   have to pay a penalty.
☐ may   ☐ will not   be entitled to a refund of part of the finance charge.

See your contract documents for any additional information about nonpayment, default, any required repayment in full before the scheduled date, and prepayment refunds and penalties.

____________
e means an estimate

Additional credit terms are defined as follows:

*Credit insurance*—You can pay premiums for life insurance, disability insurance, or property insurance. You can buy life insurance to pay off the credit balance in case you die before completing payments. You can buy disability insurance to pay the monthly payments if you should have an accident or become ill and are unable to work. You can buy insurance on the property you put up as collateral, usually a car. Such insurance will pay for the cost of repairing or replacing the property if it becomes damaged or destroyed. Creditors may or may not require you to obtain such insurance. The credit contract will tell you whether or not the creditor requires such insurance or whether or not you can refuse to buy such insurance.

*Collateral*—Creditors may take a security interest in some of your property. They may require you to put up your car or furniture as collateral. They may take a mortgage on your home. If you fail to pay back the credit, the creditor may be able to take such property from you by repossessing it or foreclosing on it.

*Default*—When you miss one payment or fail to make several payments you will be in default. This means that the creditors can try and collect everything you owe, including, in some cases, their costs in attempting to collect from you.

*Rebating*—If you pay off the balance of the loan or contract before the final due date, or if you go in default, the creditor must rebate (pay back to you) a part of the finance charge. The finance charge includes the cost of interest over the entire period of the credit transaction. If the account does not last that long a time, a portion of the unearned finance charge needs to be rebated to you. How much? The creditor usually computes the rebate interest by using a table of rates called the "Rule of 78's."

*Cosigner*—A creditor may want someone in addition to you to sign the credit agreement because you alone may not have a satisfactory credit rating. A cosigner has the responsibility to pay your debt if you do not pay it.

## Claims and Defenses

*What if I sign a retail installment contract and buy something and it doesn't work? Can I refuse to pay the creditor for it?*

Yes. Usually, a seller assigns (transfers) an installment contract to a bank or financial company. The law allows you to refuse to pay either party. The contract itself will contain a notice that advises you that you may assert your rights against any holder of the contract, which includes anyone who demands the installment payments from you.

*What if I obtain a loan and buy something with the money and it doesn't work?  Can I refuse to pay the lender?*

Only in two limited situations: Either the seller has to refer you to the bank or loan company, or the lender has to have some affiliation or connection with the seller (like common ownership or control).  These situations do not arise that often, and usually you will have to pay the lender.

*What if I use a credit card to buy something and it doesn't work?  Can I refuse to pay the creditor for it?*

Yes, in most situations.  If you buy directly from a store and use that store's credit card (like Sears or Dayton's or others), you can refuse to pay.  If you buy from a store and use a credit card from a bank (Mastercharge or VISA) or from another creditor (like American Express, Shoppers Charge, and others), you can refuse to pay for the defective goods if: (1) you first contact the seller and give that merchant a chance to solve the problem, and (2) the goods or services cost more than fifty dollars and you bought them in Minnesota or within 100 miles of your home.

*What if I receive my charge account bill and have some questions about it?  What can I do?*

If you think your bill is wrong or you have some questions about it, the Federal Fair Credit Billing Act requires a credit card company to investigate and respond to your inquiry.  All you need do is write the creditor, note your account number, and explain your question or problem.


## Use of Credit

*Why would I use credit?*

You may want to buy certain goods now without waiting to save the money to pay cash.  You may need to buy a car on credit because you will not be able to pay thousands of dollars in cash to pay for a car.  You may need credit to get through an emergency, like medical expenses.  You may want to use credit because it is convenient.  It may be easier than paying cash.  You may plan to buy something on credit so that in case you have problems with it you can refuse to pay for it in certain situations until the problem is solved.  Credit can be overused and should only be used if you have a good reason.

*Who can obtain credit?*

Anyone can obtain credit who has the ability to pay for it.  Creditors extend credit to consumers who have the money to pay later on the contract, loan, credit card, or mortgage.  A federal law entitled the Equal Credit Opportunity Act prohibits creditors from discriminating against and refusing to extend credit to consumers because of their sex, marital status, race, color, religion, national origin, age (over eighteen), or welfare income. Creditors can take into account a consumer's income and ability to pay in determining whether or not credit should be extended.

*What happens if a creditor denies a consumer credit?*

A creditor who refuses you credit must notify you within thirty days after your request that:

**1.** the credit has been denied, and

**2.** the reasons why you were denied credit, or a notice that you can find out why if you write to the creditor within sixty days and ask.

Typical reasons why creditors may deny you credit include temporary or irregular employment, insufficient income, excessive other credit, no property owned, or poor credit rating.

*Where can I obtain credit for personal use?*

You can obtain credit cards from retailers, banks, or financial institutions. You can sign retail installment contracts with a seller. You can obtain cash loans from banks and credit unions and small loan companies, and industrial loan and thrift companies. You can obtain home mortgages through a savings and loan company and banks.

*Are student loans available for continued education after high school?*

Yes. Loans are available at low interest rates to assist you in paying for your education after high school. There are no payments that you need to make while you are in school; payments start after you graduate or are out of school.

*When I obtain credit what should I consider?*

Your ability to pay it back, your current income, your current debts, the number and amount of monthly credit payments, and the amount of the finance charge. Before you obtain credit, the disclosure form will tell you the cost of credit and monthly payments. Read and understand these and the other terms before you sign.

*What is a credit rating?*

Most consumers have a credit rating based upon their past credit record. A rating is assigned by a credit reporting agency that collects and reports credit information. A credit rating is affected by the timing of making payments. If you usually pay late, you will have a poor credit rating. Creditors rely on these ratings and your current income and debts in deciding whether to extend you credit.

*How can I establish a credit rating?*

By using credit when you can and paying your bills on time. You have to build a credit record. You may start with credit cards and then establish that you can use these cards responsibly. Later, you will be able to obtain more credit.

*Who has access to my credit record?*

1. You do. You can contact your local credit reporting agency and ask about your rating (when you establish one).

2. Any creditor to which you have applied for credit.

3. A potential employer to whom you have applied.

4. An insurance company for insurance policy purposes.

*What if the information contained in my credit record is wrong?*

You can correct it. The Federal Fair Credit Reporting Act permits you first to ask that the credit reporting agency reinvestigate your credit record. If that does not correct the inaccuracy, you have a right to submit your own explanation (usually around 100 words) to the credit bureau, which then adds your explanation to your credit record.


## COLLECTION

*How does a creditor collect a debt from a debtor?*

Debts are collected in a variety of ways:

1. By the creditor

2. By a collection agency

3. By repossessing property

4. By suing the debtor, getting a judgment, and enforcing the judgment by garnishment, execution, or by enforcing a lien.


### By the Creditor

*What can a creditor say or do to collect a debt?*

A creditor can make reasonable efforts to collect. Reasonable efforts include collection letters and telephone calls that demand payment. These efforts cannot be unreasonable and cannot include harassing contacts, telephone calls late at night, obscene language, threats to have a debtor arrested, contacts with an employer claiming the debtor is a "deadbeat" (someone who refuses to pay debts for no good reason), contacts with relatives or friends demanding they pay, or notices that look like governmental documents or legal process.

## By a Collection Agency

*What can a collection agency do to collect a debt?*

A creditor can hire a collection agency to collect a debt from you. The Federal Fair Debt Collection Practices Act restricts what a collection agency can and cannot do. A collection agency can only telephone you between 8:00 A.M. and 9:00 P.M. and must first identify who he or she is and why he or she is calling you before demanding payment. This collection agent cannot lie to you or threaten you if you refuse to pay. The collection agency can contact your employer to verify if you are working there. You can stop these contacts with your employer if you advise the agent that your employer has a policy that prohibits such calls. The collection agency can contact your relatives and friends to discover where you are living. The collection agent, like a creditor, cannot do anything unreasonable.

*What if I dispute a debt with a collection agency?*

You can send a written note explaining your dispute, and the collection agency must then stop collecting from you until it is determined that your debt is valid.

## By Repossessing Property

*Under what circumstances can a creditor repossess property?*

If you put up some of your property as collateral to obtain credit, a creditor may be able to repossess (take) that property if you fail to pay.

*How can a creditor repossess?*

First, you can voluntarily turn your property over to them. You may not want it or may not be able to pay for it.

Or creditors can repossess some of your property without your consent. A creditor will be able to repossess your car without notifying you by using a duplicate key or by having it towed away. The law permits this type of repossession as long as the creditor does not breach the peace or any law in the process.

Creditors can also repossess by going to court. You can refuse to allow them to repossess your property. This will be most effective for property in your home or garage. The law prohibits them from breaking into your home or garage and taking your property. They must first go to court, which gives you notice of their intent and an opportunity to hire an attorney and defend the lawsuit.

*How can I get my property back after it has been repossessed?*

You can make the payments you missed plus any expenses incurred by the creditor in repossessing the goods. You can contact the creditor and discuss some compromise agreement to solve the problem.

*What happens after repossession?*

The creditor usually must sell the property at a sale and give you notice of such sale.

*Will I owe the creditor anything after such a sale?*

You might. If the total amount of credit you obtained to buy the goods was less than $3,000, and if you owe the creditor more than the creditor obtained at the sale, the creditor can sue you for this difference. For example, if you obtained a $2,200 loan, paid the creditor only $500, and then defaulted, and if the creditor has repossessed your car incurring $100 in expenses and sold your car for $1,400, the creditor could sue you for $400 ($2,200 – $500 + $100 – $1,400 = $400). This $400 is called a "deficiency" claim. Otherwise, the creditor satisfies your debt by repossessing your property and you owe nothing more.

## By Suing the Debtor

*How does a creditor sue a debtor?*

**creditor:** the person who has the right to receive payment.

**debtor:** the person who has the duty to pay the debt.

Through a lawsuit. The **creditor** serves a summons and complaint on a debtor demanding payment. If the **debtor** does not answer and deny this complaint, the creditor will obtain judgment. If the debtor does answer and deny the complaint, the matter will go to trial and a judge or jury will decide whether the creditor is entitled to a judgment. The amount of any judgment will equal what the debtor owes the creditor.

*How does a creditor enforce a judgment?*

One way is by a wage garnishment. This is a legal process that allows a creditor to obtain money directly from a debtor's employer. The creditor serves notice on the debtor and the employer, and the employer will usually then deduct from the debtor's salary a portion of the judgment and pay that over to the creditor.

*How much salary will be withheld?*

That depends upon how much you earn. The law exempts (protects) the bulk of your salary. The employer must pay you the greater of seventy-five percent of your take home pay, or forty times the federal minimum wage rate times the number of weeks in the pay period.

*Are there other types of garnishment?*

Yes. A creditor can serve a garnishment upon a debtor's checking account or savings account. The bank or financial institution will pay the amount of the judgment from the account to a creditor less any exempt wages in that account that were deposited within twenty days of the garnishment and all public assistance (welfare) moneys in the account that were deposited within sixty days of the garnishment. Some difficulties arise when such exempt money is mixed with other dollars in the account, but such exempt money remains protected even if mixed.

*Are there other ways to enforce a judgment?*

Yes. A creditor can obtain a writ of execution from a court and have a sheriff seize some of the debtor's property. A creditor can place a judgment lien on real property (house), which will not force the debtor to sell the home but will force the payment of the judgment at the time the home is sold.

*What personal property can the sheriff seize?*

The law protects most personal property. You know that the law allows a creditor to repossess some of your property that you put up as collateral to obtain credit. You also know that the law exempts the bulk of wages from collection. The law also allows you to keep some of your property no matter how far you go into debt. The law exempts the following property:

1. $3,000 worth of personal and household goods such as clothing, furniture, appliances, televisions, stereos. This $3,000 is present value, not replacement cost or original cost.

2. $2,000 worth of a car (present value).

3. A house or mobile home residence.

4. The earnings of a minor child (under eighteen).

5. Other property such as farm equipment, office equipment, and sources of income like public assistance.

*Are there other ways a creditor can collect payment?*

Yes. Some creditors will be able to obtain a lien on a debtor's property. A lien allows a creditor to hold or claim a debtor's property until the creditor receives payment. Some liens will also allow a creditor to force a sale and obtain payment from the sale proceeds.

*How may a seller obtain a lien?*

The typical lien arises when a creditor provides some service to a consumer or performs some work on the debtor's property and the debtor fails to pay.

For example, a mechanic who repairs a car may claim a lien for such work.  If you refuse to pay for the repairs, the mechanic could keep your car until you paid.  There are other types of liens, including a lien a tradesperson will have on your house for services performed (like plumbing work and installing a water pump).  Usually, the creditor does not have to sue and obtain a judgment before enforcing a lien.

## HELP!

*What can I do to help myself with problems I have with sellers and creditors?*

You can do much to help yourself.  You have rights and remedies and may be able to solve many of your own problems.  You will need help with some of your problems, particularly major ones and lawsuits.  But you can solve many of your own problems.

You can best assert your rights by complaining and demanding that something be done.  There are several things you can and should do.

1. Keep a record of your problems.  Makes notes about contacts and conversations you have with sellers or creditors.

2. Keep a record of your expenses and damages. Make notes of what things cost, including repairs and expenses.

3. First complain to the person you think can help you, and continue complaining until you reach the top management of the seller or creditor.

4. Prepare what you want to say so that you will not forget something important and so that you can present your best case.

5. Explain the facts of what happened.

6. Explain what you want.  Specify your demands.

7. Remain calm and sound reasonable.

8. Insist on a reason why your problem cannot be solved;  continue to insist until you are given a reason that makes common sense.

*Are there government agencies that can help me?*

Sometimes.  There are federal and state and sometimes local government consumer services departments that help consumers.  However, these agencies ordinarily do not solve individual problems.

*Are there private agencies?*

Yes.  Many communities have a Better Business Bureau that may help consumers.  Other communities have local newspapers or television stations that help investigate and negotiate a complaint between a consumer and a seller or creditor.

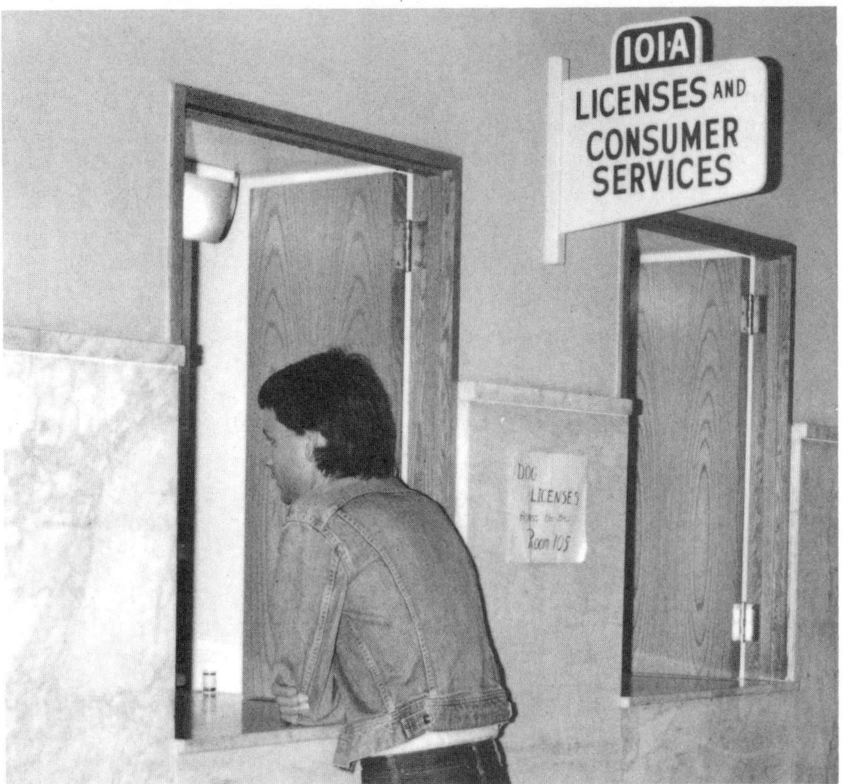


*If you have a consumer problem, ask for help.*

*Who else can help?*

An attorney.  You should contact an attorney if you are sued or if you have a significant problem you cannot solve.

## EXCESSIVE DEBTS

*What can be done when a consumer goes so far in debt that he or she cannot pay bills?*

There are several avenues of relief.  That consumer can:

1. Contact the creditors and discuss the problem and arrange to make reduced payments.

2. Seek help from a budget counseling service through a local social service agency or consumer credit counseling bureau.  These agencies will help you with your budget and advise you how to balance it.

3. Consider a Chapter XIII Wage Earner Plan.

4. Consider bankruptcy as a last resort.

*What is a Chapter XIII wage earner plan?*

This is a plan that you and your attorney submit to a federal court officer. The plan has you pay your income to a federal officer who, in turn, pays your creditors a reduced amount, prohibits these creditors from collecting any more money from you, and returns the balance of your income to you. This plan makes most sense when the consumer has a steady job and excessive debts.

*What is bankruptcy?*

Bankruptcy is a federal proceeding that discharges (cancels) all your debts. You, through an attorney, file a bankruptcy petition that lists all your property, income, and debts. The bankruptcy officer determines which property you retain and distributes any money you have to your creditors. Then the officer discharges your obligations to make any more payments on such debts and you start over again, debt free. Bankruptcy is usually a last resort for those consumers who have little income and high debts.

## PROBLEM 1

Chris (who is over eighteen) is home one afternoon. A salesperson, Dale, visits the home to sell an All Clean vacuum cleaner. Chris invites Dale to demonstrate the machine. Dale vacuums the living room rug and then unhooks the vacuum bag and shows Chris the amount of dirt collected. There is a substantial amount of dirt in the bag, but part of that dirt was already in the bag from a previous use in another consumer's home. Dale then tells Chris that the All Clean machine is the best vacuum cleaner made, that its motor will last at least twenty years, and that the machine comes with a 100% guarantee. Chris agrees to buy one and signs a sales contract for $400. Chris did not receive a "notice" of cancellation. Dale keeps the contract and returns the next day with the new machine and Chris pays $400 in a certified check. Dale hands Chris a copy of a warranty stating that the All Clean Company will only be responsible for repairing or replacing the vacuum cleaner at its option if the consumer does not abuse or misuse the machine.

One month later, the vacuum cleaner gradually starts to lose suction, and after another month the motor fails to work. Chris calls Dale and Dale tells Chris that Chris must have "misused" the machine and refuses to repair it or replace it.

1. Can Chris cancel the sales contract even though three days have passed?

2. Is the presence of the extra dirt in the vacuum bag a deceptive sales practice? Why?

3. Are the statements "best vacuum cleaner" and "the motor will last at least twenty years" opinions or express oral warranties? Why?

**4.** Is the statement "100% guarantee" a deceptive sales practice?  An express oral warranty?  Why?

**5.** What remedies does Chris have to solve this problem?

**6.** What would you advise Chris to do?


## PROBLEM 2

What did you or your family buy over the last year?  Did some sales practice deceive you?  Did something you bought become defective?  Did a seller or manufacturer refuse to honor a warranty?

Did you or your family have any problems in obtaining or using credit over the past months or years?  Did any creditor try to collect any debt from you or your family?

Take one or more of these situations that happened to you or your family, apply the rights and remedies discussed in this chapter, and determine how you would have gone about trying to solve the problem.


## PROBLEM 3

Pat (who is over eighteen) wants to buy a car that costs $1,200.  Contact the following creditors and ask them what interest rate they would charge if Pat were to obtain $1,200 credit to buy the car:

**1.** A car dealer

**2.** A bank

**3.** A small loan company

**4.** An "Industrial Loan and Thrift Company"

**5.** A credit union

Tell the creditors that you are doing a project for your class.

# 8

# ALCOHOL, TOBACCO, DRUGS AND MARIJUANA

It is an obvious fact that young people of your age are more interested in participating in adult activities than ever before since Minnesota lowered the age for the legal consumption of alcohol to nineteen for most purposes. (This age was determined in 1976 when the legislature raised the age from eighteen to nineteen. See Minn. Stat. §340.035.) It is another fact that a great many adults drink or smoke, or do both. Most young people are very interested in these activities and some may already be experimenting with them. It is for this reason that a separate chapter on alcohol and tobacco has been added, so you might understand your rights and responsibilities while engaging in these activities as a minor, and later as an adult.

It is an unfortunate fact that some young people have become involved with drugs. This fact affects *all* young people's lives in some way or another. The purpose of the drugs and marijuana section of this chapter is not to moralize or sermonize but to present the legal facts regarding drugs. With all the present attention paid to "the drug problem," you must realize by now all the consequences of drug use. It is up to you to draw the conclusions that are right for your own life, which is the essence of adult responsibility.

## CONTENTS

## CASE STUDY

*Jerry is asked to let some classmates use his car for an hour. He knows that these particular persons have been involved in the local drug underground, and he subsequently learns that they may be meeting in his car to distribute amphetamines ("speed"). He doesn't want to get involved but he gives them his keys.*

1. Does Jerry have any legal responsibility to report the meeting? (A clue to possible answers may be found in Minn. Stat. §609.05(1))

2. Are there other obligations beyond possible legal responsibility that might compel Jerry to act?

---

### SELF-QUIZ

Before you read the chapter, try the following quiz. Answer each question as best you can, based on your general knowledge. When you have read the chapter, go back to see whether or not you have changed your mind about any of the answers.

1. An alcoholic beverage is any drink that can make people drunk when taken in large quantities. _______ True _______ False

2. Both malt liquor and 3.2 beer are intoxicating liquors by legal definition. _______ True _______ False

3. Strong beer, wine, and "hard liquor" are intoxicating liquors by legal definition. _______ True _______ False

4. Under Minnesota law it is legal for people under nineteen to drink 3.2 beer with their parents both at home and at an establishment selling 3.2 beer. _______ True _______ False

5. Any minor who attempts to buy liquor or even enters a liquor store to attempt to buy can be charged with a criminal act called a misdemeanor. _______ True _______ False

6. Both owners and clerks of a liquor store or bar can be charged with illegal selling of liquor or 3.2 beer to minors. _______ True _______ False

7. The owner of a liquor store or bar cannot lose his or her liquor license but can have the license suspended if convicted of selling liquor to minors. _______ True _______ False

8. If an individual gets drunk and injures another person in a fight or vehicle accident, the seller of the liquor could be sued and forced to pay for all damages the buyer causes. _______ True _______ False

9. If a friend over nineteen gives a minor either liquor or 3.2 beer, the law treats this as a sale of liquor or 3.2 beer. _______ True _______ False

10. Minors can be charged with a misdemeanor if they lie about or falsify their real age by using identification not their own, or if they use altered identification. _______ True _______ False

11. An adult who lends identification to a minor for purposes of buying or attempting to buy liquor can be charged with a misdemeanor.  _______ True _______ False

12. Possession of liquor or 3.2 beer means that it is in your hand or on your person.  _______ True _______ False

13. The open bottle law pertains only to the actual consumption of liquor or 3.2 beer.  _______ True _______ False

14. A minor may be charged with a misdemeanor for entering a dance hall or food establishment that serves liquor or 3.2 beer.  _______ True _______ False

15. The law forbids minors not with parents to loiter on the same premises where 3.2 beer or liquor is served unless the establishment has a separate room where alcoholic beverages are not served.  _______ True _______ False

16. You have just turned nineteen years of age and you want to celebrate. You approach a bar and the bouncer at the door asks to see your driver's license for proof of age.  You don't drive, but in anticipation of this event you show a birth certificate, a school I.D. with your birthdate on it, and a passport with your birthdate on it.  The bouncer must let you in.  _______ True _______ False

17. Anyone under eighteen who is carrying cigarettes on his or her person is breaking the law.  _______ True _______ False

18. If a doctor prescribes L.S.D., the patient may legally use it. _______ True _______ False

19. Selling drugs and giving them away are considered the same under the law.  _______ True _______ False

20. Letting a friend try your codeine cough syrup to cure a cough is illegal even though you have a doctor's prescription.  _______ True _______ False

21. Marijuana may be used in very small amounts with no violation of state law.  _______ True _______ False

22. The drug laws are written to punish pushers rather than users. _______ True _______ False

# ALCOHOL

*What is an alcoholic beverage?*

Generally, an alcoholic beverage is any drink that can make people drunk when taken in large quantities.  Minnesota law divides alcoholic beverages into two types and defines each exactly.  The first type is "nonintoxicating malt liquor;" it contains not less than one-half of 1 percent alcohol by volume and not more than 3.2 percent alcohol by weight.  (Minn. Stat. §340.001 (2)) Most people call this "3.2 beer."  The second type of alcoholic beverage is called "intoxicating liquors;" these contain more than 3.2 percent alcohol by weight.  (Minn. Stat. §340.07(2))  Intoxicating liquors include strong beer, wine, and "hard liquor."

## Buying and Drinking

*May I buy or drink 3.2 beer?*

It is a misdemeanor for anyone under nineteen to buy 3.2 beer or to drink it unless in the presence of parents. (Minn. Stat. §340.035)

*May I buy or drink hard liquor, wine, or strong beer?*

It is illegal for a minor to consume, buy, attempt to buy, have another buy for him or her, or enter a liquor store to try to buy any of these intoxicating liquors. (Minn. Stat. §340.731) All of these acts are misdemeanors. (Minn. Stat. §340.732)

**TABLE 8-1   State Drinking Ages**

### 18 YEARS OLD

1. Connecticut
2. Florida
3. Georgia
4. Hawaii
5. Iowa
6. Louisiana
7. Massachusetts
8. Montana
9. New Hampshire
10. New Jersey
11. New York
12. Rhode Island
13. Tennessee
14. Texas
15. Vermont
16. West Virginia
17. Wisconsin

### 19 YEARS OLD

1. Alabama
2. Alaska
3. Arizona
4. Idaho
5. Iowa
6. Michigan
7. Minnesota
8. Nebraska
9. Wyoming

### 20 YEARS OLD

1. Delaware
2. Maine

### 21 YEARS OLD

1. Arkansas
2. California
3. Colorado°
4. Washington D.C.°°
5. Illinois°°°
6. Indiana
7. Kansas°
8. Kentucky
9. Maryland
10. Mississippi°
11. Missouri
12. Nevada
13. New Mexico
14. North Carolina°°
15. North Dakota
16. Ohio°
17. Oklahoma°
18. Oregon
19. Pennsylvania
20. South Carolina°°
21. South Dakota°
22. Utah
23. Virginia°
24. Washington

°*Beer at 18*
°°*Beer and wine at 18*
°°°*Beer and wine at 19*

*Most liquor stores post the law regarding minors on their door.*

## Sale

*Can the person who sells me liquor get into trouble?*

Yes.  There are strict penalties that make most bar and liquor store owners careful to check the ages of their customers.  First, it is a gross misdemeanor to sell intoxicating liquor to a minor (Minn. Stat. §340.73) and a misdemeanor to sell 3.2 beer to a minor.  (Minn. Stat. §340.035)  Both the owner of the bar or liquor store and the employee who actually made the sale could be prosecuted.  (Minn. Stat. §340.941)

Second, the seller could be found guilty of "contributing to the delinquency of a minor," a misdemeanor in Minnesota.  (Minn. Stat. §260.315;  *State v. Sobelman*, 199 Minn. 323, 271 N.W. 484 (1937))

Third, the owner's license could be taken away, or at least suspended, if he or she sells liquor to a minor.  (Minn. Stat. §340.135)  This would mean that the owner would not be allowed to sell liquor any longer and would have to close up the business.  Suspension is possible even if only 3.2 beer is sold to a minor.  (Minn. Stat. §340.01;  Op.Atty.Gen., 271-B-9, January 30, 1952)

<br>

**WHAT
DO
YOU
THINK?**

What is the Dram Shop Law?

Fourth, if you get drunk and injure another person in an automobile accident or a fight, the seller of the liquor could be sued and forced to pay for all the damages you caused. (Minn. Stat. §340.95) The seller is liable because liquor was sold to you illegally, and this is true even if it was only 3.2 beer.

*If an older friend gives me a drink or buys liquor for me, can my friend get in trouble?*

Yes, the law treats this just as if it were a sale. It is a gross misdemeanor to give intoxicating liquor to a minor  (Minn. Stat. §§340.79 and .73) and a misdemeanor to give 3.2 beer to a minor. (Minn. Stat. §340.035) The friend could also be found guilty of contributing to the delinquency of a minor. (Minn. Stat. §260.315)

## Identification

*Why do I need a driver's license or state certificate to buy alcoholic beverages?*

Only a valid driver's license or current nonqualification certificate issued by the state is sufficient identification to purchase, possess, or consume alcoholic beverages.  Liquor establishments do not have to honor any other form of identification.  (Minn. Stat. §340.039)

*What can happen if I borrow somebody's identification to buy liquor?*

It is a misdemeanor to lie about your age to buy liquor, even if it is only 3.2 beer. (Minn. Stat. §§340.035 and 340.731) A friend who lends you a driver's license could also get in trouble.  It is a misdemeanor to lend a driver's license to another person.  (Minn. Stat. §171.22)

## Possession

*Can I get in trouble for just having liquor even if I'm not caught drinking?*

Just as if you commit any other violation of law, it is illegal for a person under nineteen years of age to possess intoxicating liquor or to possess 3.2 beer if you intend to consume it in any place other than your parents' home. If you are eighteen years old it is a misdemeanor punishable by a $500 fine and/or ninety days in jail. (Minn. Stat. §340.035 and Minn. Stat. §340.731)

If, however, you are under eighteen years old and you violate this statute, you are subject to arrest and jurisdiction of the juvenile court until you are twenty-one years old.

Possession does not necessarily mean that you have to have liquor in your hand; it is enough if you have control over it. (Op.Atty.Gen., 217-F-3, July 22, 1966) In addition, it is a violation of the open bottle law and a misdemeanor to have an open container of liquor in the passenger compartment of your car while it is on the road even though you have not drunk any of the bottle's contents. (Minn. Stat. §169.122)

*What about liquor in school?*

It is a misdemeanor for any person to have intoxicating liquor or nonintoxicating malt liquor on school grounds or in a school building. (Minn. Stat. §624.701)

## Bars and Restaurants

*Can I go into a place that serves liquor if I only buy food, or dance?*

While you would not be guilty of any crime, it might be illegal for the owner to allow you to do this. It is illegal for the seller to permit a minor to loiter (hang around) or to be in a room where 3.2 beer is sold unless the minor is accompanied by his or her parents. (Minn. Stat. §340.035) It is not completely clear what loitering includes here, but the statute has been interpreted to forbid holding dances for minors on the premises if 3.2 beer is sold (Op.Atty.Gen. 217-F-3, March 10, 1955); to forbid the seller to allow minors to play pinball on the premises (Op.Atty.Gen., 217-F-3, November 19, 1953); and to forbid allowing minors to stand around and smoke if beer is served on the premises. (Op.Atty.Gen., 217-F-3, June 9, 1945) On the other hand, it is legal to allow minors to attend a baseball game where 3.2 beer is sold (Op.Atty.Gen., 218-G-15, August 13, 1945) and to serve them lunches on the same premises, though not in the same room. (Op.Atty.Gen., 217-F-3, April 6, 1950) To avoid trouble with the law, many pizza places have one room in which they serve no beer, and they refuse to allow their minor customers to enter the room in which they do serve beer.

It is probably illegal for the owner of a place that sells hard liquor to allow you to enter at all, even if you do not drink or attempt to do so, if allowing you in might contribute to your delinquency, or if your parents have given the owner written notice that you are a minor. (Op.Atty.Gen., 217-F-3, September 17, 1964) However, minors can enter the premises if the sale of intoxicating liquor is not one of the main activities of the business; for example, a drug store that sells a small amount of bottled liquor can safely allow you to enter. (Op.Atty.Gen., 217-F-3, 218-J-12, December 8, 1953)

## Drunkenness

*What can happen to an older person who is drunk in public?*

Before 1971 public drunkenness was a crime. The state legislature changed that law and now persons who are intoxicated in public or who are arrested while intoxicated are taken to "detoxification centers." There they may be confined for up to seventy-two hours so that they can be sobered up and given shelter, food, and counseling. (Minn. Stat. §245A.01 and .10) However, a person who causes a disturbance or commits a crime while drunk may still be arrested and put in jail as a result. This crime is known as disorderly conduct, which makes it a misdemeanor to engage in offensive, obscene, abusive, boisterous, or noisy conduct that tends to arouse alarm, anger, or resentment in others.  (Minn. Stat. §609.72)  Driving while under the influence of alcohol remains a crime.  (Minn. Stat. §169.121)

## TOBACCO

*Is it legal for me to smoke?*

No.  Anyone under eighteen who uses tobacco may be jailed for thirty days and fined up to fifty dollars.  This includes cigarettes, cigars, pipes, and even chewing tobacco.  (Minn. Stat. §609.685)

*Teenage girls and young women make up the largest number of smokers.*

*Is it legal to give a cigarette to a friend?*

No. It is illegal to furnish (sell or give) tobacco to anyone under eighteen. You could be punished by thirty days in jail or a fine of fifty dollars. (Minn. Stat. §609.685)

*Can a person who sells me cigarettes get in trouble?*

Yes. The person would be guilty of furnishing you with tobacco and could be punished by thirty days in jail or a fine of fifty dollars. Also, persons who own or lease cigarette vending machines are required to post a large sign on them that states that it is illegal for persons under eighteen to buy cigarettes. An owner who fails to post a sign like this is guilty of a misdemeanor. (Minn. Stat. §325.765)


## DRUGS AND MARIJUANA

*What is a narcotic or dangerous drug?*

The law lists by name all of the drugs, chemicals, or medicines that it considers to be narcotics or dangerous drugs. There are too many to list here, but in general any drug that is dangerous to take without the advice of a doctor is included in the laws about narcotics and dangerous drugs. (Minn. Stat. §152.02)

*What are the most common types of drugs?*

The law divides drugs into five groups.

**Group 1**—Drugs that have no medical use and are dangerous even if given by a doctor. Examples are heroin, L.S.D., and marijuana. These drugs are grouped together by the law even though they have different effects on the person taking them, because they are all drugs that no doctor will ever prescribe to you. There is no state statute that permits doctors to prescribe these drugs.

**Group 2**—Drugs that have a medical use in a few circumstances but are very dangerous and may lead to severe physical or psychological dependence or addiction. Examples are methadone, a drug which doctors sometime give to heroin addicts instead of heroin, and morphine and other very strong painkillers, which doctors sometime give to people in great pain.

**Group 3**—Drugs that have medical uses and are less dangerous than the drugs in the previous groups but that can cause some physical addiction and severe psychological dependence if abused. Examples are amphetamines and methamphetamines (like uppers and speed) and strong barbiturates (downers).

*What are the issues relating to marijuana laws?*



**Group 4**—Drugs that have medical use and are less likely to be abused than the drugs in the previous groups but that may cause some physical or psychological dependence if abused. Examples are sedatives such as phenobarbital and paraldehyde.

**Group 5**—Drugs that have medical use and are less likely to be abused than the drugs in the previous groups. Examples are codeine cough syrups and very mild pain killers. (Minn. Stat. §§152.01 and .02)

*What does the law say about using these drugs?*

It is legal to possess and use any of these drugs except the ones in the first group, if you have a written prescription for them from your doctor. It is illegal to:

1. Sell these drugs or give them away to another person.

2. Possess these drugs without a prescription.

3 Manufacture a drug like L.S.D. or grow marijuana.

**TABLE 8-2**  Narcotics Offenses and Penalties

| OFFENSE | MINN. STAT. SECTION | FIRST NARCOTIC OFFENSE | ONE OR MORE PRIOR NARCOTIC OFFENSES |
|---|---|---|---|
| Heroin (Or any other Opium or Coco Leaf Derivative in Group 1 or 2) | | | |
| Possession | 152.15 | 5 Years/$5,000 | 10 Years/$10,000 |
| Sale or Possession with Intent to Sell | 152.15 | 15 Years/$25,000 | 1-30 Years/$50,000 |
| Obtaining by Fraud | 152.15 | 4 Years/$30,000 | 8 Years/$60,000 |
| L.S.D., Marijuana, Speed (Or any other Drug in Groups 1, 2, or 3, which is not an Opium or Coco Leaf Derivative) | | | |
| Possession | 152.15 | 3 Years/$3,000 | 6 Years/$6,000 |
| Sale or Possession with Intent to Sell | 152.15 | 5 Years/$15,000 | 1-10 Years/$30,000 |
| Obtaining by Fraud | 152.15 | 4 Years/$30,000 | 8 Years/$60,000 |
| Any Drug in Group 4 | | | |
| Possession | 152.15 | 3 Years/$3,000 | 6 Years/$6,000 |
| Sale or Possession with Intent to Sell | 152.15 | 3 Years/$10,000 | 6 Mos.-6 Years/$20,000* |
| Obtaining by Fraud | 152.15 | 4 Years/$30,000 | 8 Years/$60,000 |
| Any Drug in Group 5 | | | |
| Possession | 152.15 | 1 Year/$1,000 | 2 Years/$2,000 |
| Sale or Possession with Intent to Sell | 152.15 | 1 Year/$1,000 | 2 Years/$2,000 |
| Obtaining by Fraud | 152.15 | 4 Years/$30,000 | 8 Years/$60,000 |
| Very Small Amount of Marijuana (1.5 oz. or less) | | | |
| Possession | 152.15 | **/$100 | 90 Days/$500 |

*These are mandatory sentences; all other penalties listed are maximum.
**Participation in drug rehabilitation program.

**4.** Get drugs or even try to get drugs by altering a prescription or lying to get a prescription. (Minn. Stat. §152.11)

**5.** Drive while under the influence of drugs. (Minn. Stat. §169.121)

*Is it legal to possess a small amount of marijuana to use or give away?*

It is a petty misdemeanor to possess or to give away a small amount of marijuana. The law defines a small amount of marijuana as 1.5 ounces or less. For the first offense under this category, the court may fine you $100 and require you to participate in a drug rehabilitation program. It is also a misdemeanor to keep or allow to be kept more than .05 ounces of marijuana in the passenger compartment of an automobile. (Minn. Stat. §152.15)

Further, a second offense within two years of the first offense is a misdemeanor. The court must require this person to submit to a chemical dependency evaluation and if treatment is necessary, to place this person in treatment.

*What should I do if someone offers to give me a dangerous drug?*

It is a very serious crime for an adult to give or sell drugs to a minor; the sentence he or she would serve had the drugs been sold to an adult could be doubled. As a citizen you have a duty to report evidence of a serious crime to the proper authorities. (Minn. Stat. §152.15)

*What can happen to me if I break the drug laws?*

If you break these laws and are caught by the police, you will have to go to juvenile court. Refer to the section on juvenile court in Chapter 5 and also to Table 8-2.

*What is the state of Minnesota doing about the problem of drug dependency beyond enforcing the laws?*

The Alcohol and Drug Abuse Section of the Department of Public Welfare has been established to develop rehabilitation programs. All community mental health boards are also required to establish a detoxification program for drug dependent persons. (Minn. Stat. §§254A.03 and .08)

## PROBLEM 1

Ann Chin, a sixteen-year-old, was accompanying her parents and a twelve-year-old sister to the local pizza parlor. Ann's dad ordered a pitcher of beer and shared it with Ann's mother. Ann and her sister each had a small glass of beer.

1. Has Ann broken a law by consuming beer?

2. Has Ann's sister broken a law?

3. Has Ann's father broken a law?

4. Has the owner broken a law?

5. Has the salesperson who sold or served the beer broken a law?

6. How would the situation change if Ann and her sister consumed hard liquor?

## PROBLEM 2

Joe, seventeen years of age, borrowed an automobile from his friend, Sheryl, and went to a local tavern where, with the aid of a falsified driver's license, he was served several drinks containing bourbon whiskey.  While there he met Sally, age nineteen.

Upon leaving the tavern they drove to a nearby secluded area where they shared a marijuana cigarette that Joe had brought with him.  As they pulled away from the parking area they were stopped by a police officer who observed that the taillight on the automobile was burned out.  He asked Joe to get out of the car, examined his driver's license, and talked to him for a few minutes.  Then, with the aid of a flashlight, the officer made a careful search of the car and uncovered some capsules that later proved to contain heroin.  The officer also found the "roach" from the marijuana cigarette and, observing that both Joe and Sally were somewhat unsteady, arrested them. The officer then searched Sally's purse, finding some amphetamine capsules. Joe claims that he knows nothing about the heroin capsules and that they must belong to Sheryl, the owner of the car.  Sally says that she got the amphetamine capsules with a doctor's prescription.

1.  With what crimes may Joe or Sally be charged?

# 9
# LIFESTYLES

This chapter deals with many various topics of interest to young people. At first, the chapter was entitled "Recreation," since it dealt with many areas that would seem enjoyable, such as motorcycles, boats, hunting, guns, and movies. But this chapter also discusses cars, insurance, jobs, and curfew, which for many young people are not topics of recreation but ways of life. Consequently, the topics in this chapter best describe the areas that intimately affect the lifestyles of younger people today.

## CASE STUDY

*Martha, who is seventeen years old, and some of her high school friends, decide to go on a hunting trip to northern Minnesota. She drives her 1967 Chevrolet and lets Carmen, age sixteen, who has an instructional permit, drive while Martha sits in the back seat with Harriet and has a few beers. A highway patrolwoman stops the car for speeding and sees a rifle and some empty beer cans in the back seat. She asks Carmen for her license but is told by Martha that she, Martha, was teaching Carmen how to drive. The*

## CONTENTS

*patrolwoman examines the tires of the car and finds less than 1/16 of an inch depth of tread.*

1. What charges can be brought against Carmen?

2. What charges can be brought against Martha?

3. Can Carmen be forced to take a breath test?

4. If she refuses, what can happen?

5. If the policewoman decides to issue tickets, must Carmen and Martha sign the tickets?

6. Can the rifle be confiscated?

---

**SELF-QUIZ**

Before you read the chapter, try the following quiz. Answer each question as best you can, based on your general knowledge. When you have read the chapter, go back to see whether or not you have changed your mind about any of the answers.

1. I must have a license for any vehicle I drive, except a snowmobile. ______ True ______ False

2. I may drive unaccompanied when I have an instructional driver's permit. ______ True ______ False

3. The requirements for obtaining a motorcycle license are the same as for obtaining a license for driving an automobile. ______ True ______ False

4. It is O.K. to lend my license to a friend who wants to drive a car. ______ True ______ False

5. It is illegal to store an open bottle of liquor in the glove compartment of the car. ______ True ______ False

6. Under the Implied Consent Law, a police officer can force you to take a breath test if there are reasonable grounds to believe that you are drunk. ______ True ______ False

7. If highways or roads are slippery or snowy, it is the law that I must drive slower than the posted speed limit. ______ True ______ False

8. Signing a traffic ticket constitutes an admission of guilt. ______ True ______ False

9. Driving a car without basic insurance is a misdemeanor. ______ True ______ False

10. It is against the law to hitchhike. ______ True ______ False

11. Even if I cross the street illegally, the law says the driver of a car must yield the right of way. ______ True ______ False

12. The bicycle registration system is set up to protect bicycle owners. ______ True ______ False

13. It is not illegal to ride my bicycle on the sidewalk or road. ______ True ______ False

14. The law says an employer may not hire anyone under sixteen to work during the school year. ______ True ______ False

**15.** An employer who pays an employee less than minimum wage is breaking the law. _______ True _______ False

**16.** It is illegal for a minor to own a gun. _______ True _______ False

**17.** A minor who is under sixteen must have a certificate and parents' consent before hunting. _______ True _______ False

**18.** A hunter may have his or her license revoked immediately for hunting while intoxicated. _______ True _______ False

**19.** It is illegal to go to an X-rated movie if I am under eighteen. _______ True _______ False

**20.** If I own a dog, state law requires that I license it. _______ True _______ False

## DRIVER'S LICENSE

*For what kinds of vehicles do I need a license?*

You must have a license to drive every motorized vehicle except a snowmobile.

*Am I entitled to a driver's license as soon as I reach legal age?*

No. As you read this section, it is best to remember that a driver's license is a privilege extended by the state to its citizens and not a right. You must qualify to be licensed to drive a motor vehicle by meeting certain requirements. Then you must obey the rules and conditions under which your license is granted or the state has the right to revoke that privilege.

*How do I become eligible for a license?*

If you are under sixteen you are not eligible. Further, if you are under eighteen, have not successfully completed a course in driver's education, including both classroom and behind-the-wheel instructions, and do not have approval from a parent or guardian, you are not eligible.

*What is an instructional permit? How do I get one?*

If you are to learn how to drive, you must be allowed to practice driving. An instructional permit allows you to drive for a period of twelve months. A licensed adult or your driver's training instructor must be in the seat beside you, and you must have your permit with you. If you are fifteen you can drive only with your driver's training instructor or your parents. To get a permit, you must do the following:

1. Fill out an application blank.

2. Have the application signed by one of your parents.

3. Pay a fee.

4. Prove that you are fifteen and enrolled in an approved behind-the-wheel driver's education course, or that you are between sixteen and eighteen and have taken such a course and passed it, or that you are over eighteen.

5. Pass an eye test.

6. Pass a test to show that you can read and understand traffic signs and that you know the traffic laws.

7. Have a color picture of yourself taken for your permit. (Minn. Stat. §171.05, .06, and .13.)

*Are the requirements for a motorcycle instructional permit the same?*

Generally they are the same for a regular instructional permit. If you are under eighteen, you must successfully complete a two-wheeled vehicle driver's safety course and meet all the other requirements for a regular instructional permit. The instructional permit is valid for forty-five days and is renewable. (Minn. Stat. §169.974) While driving on a motorcycle instructional permit, you may not carry passengers, drive at night, drive on an interstate freeway, or drive without wearing protective headwear.

*How can I get a regular driver's license?*

1. Fill out an application.

2. Pay the required fee.

3. Have a colored picture taken for your license.

4. Prove that you are sixteen and have successfully completed an approved driver education course, or that you are eighteen.

5. Pass an eye test.

6. Pass a test showing that you can read and understand highway signs and that you know the traffic laws. This is not necessary if you have a valid instructional permit.

7. Pass a driver's test showing that you can control a car or a motorcycle properly.

8. Take any other physical or mental test that the Minnesota commissioner of Public Safety finds necessary to decide whether or not you would be a safe driver. (Minn. Stat.§171.04, .06 and .13)

*Are there any other kinds of licenses?*

A person between fifteen and sixteen who otherwise qualifies may be issued a restricted license for farm work to help her parents, may only drive close to the farm, and may only drive during the day. Other restricted licenses may be given to people who have a physical problem. If your license requires you to wear eye glasses when driving, it is illegal to disobey this restriction. (Minn. Stat. §171.041.09)

*If I am under sixteen, can I get an auto license if I need one for special medical or personal reasons?*

A 1975 law states that anyone between the ages of fifteen and sixteen, otherwise qualified, may hold a license if he or she needs one for "personal or family medical reasons." (Minn. Stat. §171.042) The statute does not expand on the quoted words, but the intent of this law is probably to enable young persons to transport family members to and from medical institutions.

*Do I need a special license to drive a motorcycle?*

Yes. A special endorsement is required. This means that your license to drive a car will be marked to show that you may also drive a motorcycle. You may apply at any time. The examiner will give you a driving test to see if you can drive a motorcycle skillfully. (Minn. Stat. §169.974) You must also take a written test and possess the necessary motorcycle instruction permit.

*What else do I need to know about motorcycles?*

Under current statutory definition, a motorcycle includes motor scooters and motorized bikes (mopeds). All of the rules pertaining to special endorsement and instructional permits apply to these vehicles as well. (Minn. Stat. §169.014) If you are under eighteen and possess an endorsement or instructional permit for a motorcycle, you must wear protective headgear (helmets). Further, all drivers, regardless of their age, must either wear protective eye gear or equip the bike with a windshield. Over the age of eighteen, you need not wear headgear. Finally, cyclists are required to burn their headlights at all times while their vehicle is in operation, both night and day. If a driver takes a passenger, that passenger must ride on a secure seat and must not obstruct the driver's vision. (Minn. Stat. §169.974)

*What should I do if I lose my license?*

You must prove that you have lost it, fill out a form, and pay a fee. You will then get a new "duplicate" license. You must also apply for a duplicate license if your old license becomes so worn that it is impossible to read. (Minn. Stat. §171.10)

*What should I do if I move?*

Within thirty days after moving you must apply for a duplicate license, turn in your old license, and pay a fee. You must also do this if you change your name, say when a person chooses to change their name upon marriage. (Minn. Stat. §171.11)

*What are the limits on the use of my driver's license?*

It is illegal to:

1. Possess a canceled, revoked, suspended, fictitious, or altered license

2. Lend your license to anyone else

3. Borrow anyone's license and use it as your own

4. Change or alter your license or make a counterfeit license (Minn. Stat. §171.22)

*What will happen if I do any of these things?*

Violations of these rules in the preceding list are treated as misdemeanors, and if you are under eighteen, you would have to appear in juvenile traffic court (see the section on juvenile court in Chapter 5). If you are eighteen or over, you would go to adult traffic court. (Minn. Stat. §260.193)

*What can happen if I take a friend's driving test or written exam?*

Both of you have committed a misdemeanor. You would have to appear in juvenile traffic court. Again, consult the juvenile court section in Chapter 5. (Minn. Stat. §§172.22 and 260.193)

*What can happen if I drive without a license?*

Driving without a license is illegal, and you would have to appear in juvenile traffic court. (Minn. Stat. §§171.04, 260.193)


## MOTOR VEHICLES

*What is a motor vehicle?*

A motor vehicle is any self-propelled vehicle that can carry people or property. In other words, motorcycles, scooters, mini-bikes, dirt bikes, go-carts, motorized bicycles, and similar small vehicles must follow the same rules as automobiles. (Minn. Stat. §168.011, Subd. 4 and §169.01, Subd. 3)

*Can I drive my mini-bike on the streets?*

Not unless it is registered. This means that you must apply for license plates and pay a tax. (Minn. Stat. §§168.012 and 168.09) Violation of this rule is a misdemeanor. (Minn. Stat. §168.36) The bike must also have proper seats, handlebars, foot rests, horns, and other equipment. (Minn. Stat. §169.974) Many mini-bikes don't have this kind of equipment. If the bike can't travel at speeds over twenty-five miles per hour, it can't be driven on the streets without a large orange, triangular, slow-moving vehicle emblem. (Minn. Stat. §169.522)

*Do these same laws apply to motorized bicycles?*

You may not drive a motorized bicycle without possessing a valid driver's license unless the person has obtained a motorized bicycle operator's permit from the commissioner of Public Safety. (Minn. Stat. §171.02) A permit to operate a motorized bicycle may be issued to anyone who is fifteen years of age and has passed a written exam and a driver's safety course. Motorized bikes are not allowed on bicycle paths or bicycle lanes or upon the sidewalk. All lighting and brake equipment that is necessary for motorcycles are required for motor bikes. (Minn. Stat. §169.223)

*The rules that apply to automobiles include mopeds.*

*Can I get into trouble if I customize my car with headers, glass pack mufflers, spotlights, heavy rear springs, and similar equipment?*

All of these items are probably illegal. The law requires normal mufflers and prohibits cut-outs, by-passes, and similar devices. (Minn. Stat. §169.69) There is also a legal limit on the amount of noise a vehicle can make, regardless of the kind of muffler it has, and the owner is responsible for reducing the noise level to comply with the law. (Minn. Stat. §§169.691 and .692) It is also illegal to put such stiff rear springs on your car that the middle of the rear bumper is more than twenty inches above the ground. (Minn. Stat. §169.73) Most spotlights, flashing lights, and colored lights are also forbidden. (Minn. Stat. §168.64) So are horns that make any sounds other than those normally made by a horn. (Minn. Stat. §169.68) Violation of these rules is a petty misdemeanor. (Minn. Stat. §169.89) It is also a petty misdemeanor to "drive, move or cause to be driven or moved, a motor vehicle with unsafe tires." (Minn. Stat. §169.721)

*What are unsafe tires?*

Unsafe tires are defined as tires with any of the following defects:

**1.** Ply or cord exposed

**2.** Noticeable bump, bulge, or separation

**3.** Tread design depth less than 1/16 of an inch measured at three equidistant places

**4.** Tread worn to a level of tread wear indicators in two grooves at three places

5. Tires marked "Not for Highway Use" or "Unsafe"

6. Deep cracks, cuts, or snags, exposing the cord

7. Tires regrooved or retreaded below 1/16 of an inch depth  (Minn. Stat. §169.723)

Tires may be checked by law enforcement officers, by visual inspection, or by use of a simple measuring gauge. (Minn. Stat. §169.725) It is also illegal to sell vehicles with unsafe tires as it is defined.  (Minn. Stat. §169.726)

*Must I wear a seat belt?*

At the present time, there is no law requiring you to wear your seat belt. However, it is the law that all cars built after 1964 must be equipped with seat belts on the left and right front seats.  (Minn. Stat. §169.685)

*Can I get a ticket for an equipment violation even if my lights just stopped working and I didn't know about it.*

Yes.  The law requires certain equipment on all cars operated on the road and makes it illegal to drive without it;  it is not necessary that you know that the equipment is faulty.  If your lights had just burned out, however, a police officer would probably only give you a warning or "fix-it" ticket.

*What is the open bottle law?*

The open bottle law makes it a misdemeanor to have an open bottle or can of hard liquor or beer in a car on the street.  Any opened container must be kept in the trunk.  You are breaking the law even if the container is in the glove compartment or if the person with the open bottle is a passenger.  (Minn. Stat. §169.122)

*What is the implied consent law?*

The implied consent law says that if you drive a motor vehicle, you have agreed to have your blood, breath, or urine tested under certain circumstances to determine whether you are driving while drunk.  If a police officer has reasonable grounds to believe that you were driving while under the influence of alcohol or with .10 or more blood alcohol, you can be asked to take a test if you have been arrested for drunk driving, or if you have been involved in an accident.  If you refuse to take a test, the police can't force you to do it, but your driver's license will be revoked for six months. (Minn. Stat. §169.123)  If you decide to take the test and you fail, you will be subject to criminal penalties and may have your license suspended for ninety days.

*What is the basic speed law?*

The basic speed law simply says that you may not drive faster than is "reasonable and prudent" under existing conditions regardless of any specific speed limit.  It also says that you shall drive as slow as is necessary to avoid hitting a pedestrian or other vehicle that is also obeying the law.  This means that you must drive slower than the posted speed limit if the roads are slippery or snowy, or if there are any other conditions that might make it dangerous to go faster.  If the speed limit is posted in a municipality it is the legal maximum; in other than a municipality the posted limit is that legally presumed to be safe and reasonable.  If you are arrested for speeding outside of a municipality, the fact that you were driving faster than the posted limit would be evidence against you, and you would have to prove that it was safe to drive as fast as you did.  (Minn. Stat. §§169.14(4) and (5))  The transportation commissioner of Minnesota has issued an executive order declaring the speed limit to be 55 m.p.h. by authority of the Fuel Conservation Highway Speed Reduction Act.  (Minn. Stat. §169.141)

*Do I have to sign a traffic ticket even if I'm not guilty?*

Yes.  When you sign a traffic ticket you do not admit that you are guilty.  Your signature only means that you promise to appear in traffic court.  If you refuse to sign, the police officer cannot release you, and you will be taken into custody immediately.  (Minn. Stat. §169.91(7))

*What are the "rules of the road"?*

These rules describe the way in which automobiles and other motor vehicles may be driven.  They govern speed, traffic signals, right-of-way, and many other matters.  There are too many of these laws to describe here.  Copies of the rules may be obtained from the Department of Motor Vehicles.  You must know these rules to get a driver's license.

*What should I do if I have an automobile accident?*

You must stop immediately at the scene of the accident or as close as you can without blocking traffic.  You are required by the law to stop even if the damage done is very slight.  If anyone is injured in the accident you must give first aid and call the police.  If there is any damage to property or any injury, you must give the other driver your name and address and the registration number of your automobile.  If you damage a parked car or some other kind of property, you must attempt to notify the owner.  Failure to stop and do these things is a misdemeanor and you will not be given a ticket but taken into custody by the police if you are caught.  (Minn. Stat. §§169.09 and .91(5))  If the accident causes death, personal injury, or property damage of $300 or more, you must also fill out a written accident report and submit it to the Minnesota commissioner of Public Safety.  If you fail to do so, it is a misdemeanor and your driver's license may be suspended.  (Minn. Stat. §§169.09 and 170.24)

*Do I have to buy automobile insurance?*

As of January 1, 1975, Minnesota's "no-fault" insurance law makes it a misdemeanor to drive your car without having certain basic insurance

---

**WHAT DO YOU THINK?**

Andrea witnessed a car accident.  One of the drivers seemed to be speeding.  Rather than give her name as a witness, she decided to walk on because she didn't want to get involved.  What do you think of this attitude?  Why do you think Andrea didn't want to get involved?  Does she have a legal duty to give her name?  A moral duty?  What are some of the differences between a legal duty and a moral duty?

coverage or to drive any car knowing it has no such coverage. Your license could be suspended for six to twelve months, and if you own the car your auto registration could be revoked for the same period. In any case, you would also be liable for the injuries you might have caused without limitation, unlike coverage under no-fault. (Minn. Stat. §65B.41) One way to understand no-fault insurance is to compare it to the well-known Blue Cross/Blue Shield insurance concept under which a person's own insurance company pays the insurance benefits directly. Under the prior "fault" theory, it was necessary to determine who caused the accident in order that the insurance company representing the person at fault could pay for the injuries caused to others. This was based on personal liability for negligent acts causing injury to another. The no-fault concept is that everyone owning or operating a motor vehicle carries insurance against injury to the owner (and injury to members of the household), payable directly to him or her by the insurance company, regardless of who caused an accident.

The no-fault law requires coverage to include $20,000 for hospital and medical expense benefits and an additional $10,000 to cover all other economic loss, such as loss of wages, funeral expenses, and survivors' loss of support in the event of a death.

Even with this no-fault law, certain circumstances are specified that would once more call into play the fault theory, permitting one person to sue another for negligently causing an accident and requiring that person to pay damages for noneconomic loss, such as pain and suffering. However, at least one of the following circumstances must result from the accident before such suits are permitted.

1. disability for more than sixty days

2. permanent injury

3. permanent disfigurement

4. death

5. medical expense exceeding $2,000

## HITCHHIKING AND PEDESTRIANS

*What is hitchhiking?*

Hitchhiking is asking the driver of a motor vehicle for a ride. (It could be a car, motor scooter, motorcycle, and the like.) It is hitchhiking whether you use your thumb, knock on car windows, or simply ask the driver.

*Is it against the law to hitchhike?*

No. It is not against the law to hitchhike, but you must obey three rules.

1. You may not hitchhike while standing in the "roadway." In most areas this means that both feet should be on the curb. If there is no curb, you should stand well off the shoulder, the area beyond the edge of the road.

*It is illegal to hitchhike on freeways.*

**2.** By order of the highway commissioner, you may not hitchhike on freeways. (Minn. Stat. §169.305)

**3.** You may not hitchhike in such a way that you block the road, interfere with traffic, or make the road dangerous for others. (Minn. Stat. §169.22, Mpls. Ord. Code Sec. 408.070, St. Paul Leg. Code Sec. 134.31, Minn. Stat. §609.74)

*What can happen to me if I violate these rules?*

If you hitchhike from the roadway you might receive a traffic ticket and would have to go to juvenile court. This violation is a misdemeanor. (See Chapter Five on the juvenile court.) (Minn. Stat. §§169.22, 260.193 and 609.74)

*What is a pedestrian?*

The law defines a pedestrian as "any person afoot." (Minn. Stat. §169.01(24))

*What is jaywalking?*

Jaywalking is the popular name for crossing a street in the middle of a block or crossing against the light.

*Do pedestrians have to obey traffic lights?*

Yes. In general you must obey the signals just as an automobile must. You cannot cross on a red light or a "Don't Walk" sign. You may start to cross the road on a green light or a "Walk" sign, and if you do, the drivers must give you the right-of-way. (Minn. Stat. §§169.06(5) and (6))

*When can I cross the street if there is no light?*

You may always cross in a marked crosswalk and if you do, drivers must yield the right-of-way to you. (Minn. Stat. §169.21(2)) If you cross other than at an intersection or a marked crosswalk, you must yield the right-of-way to automobiles. You may never cross in the middle of a block between two intersections that have traffic lights. (Minn. Stat. §169.21(3)) Even if you are crossing the street illegally, the law requires drivers to be careful to avoid hitting you. (Minn. Stat. §169.21(3))

*Can I walk in the street?*

You may not walk along or in the street or road if there are sidewalks that you could use instead. If there are no sidewalks, you can walk in the road or along the shoulder. You must stay close to the left side (face oncoming traffic) and yield the right-of-way to drivers. (Minn. Stat. §169.21(5))

## BICYCLES

*What is a bicycle?*

The law defines a bicycle as anything that is propelled by "human power" on which a person can ride, and which has either two wheels at least twenty inches in diameter, or has more wheels but is generally recognized as a bicycle (for example, a bicycle with training wheels). (Minn. Stat. §169.01(51))

*Do I have to get a license for my bicycle?*

Since March 1, 1977, the legislature has established a state-wide bicycle registration system. Bicycle owners may apply for three-year registration and a license plate. Driving your bicycle without the required license may result in the police impounding your bicycle and fining you. One of the main reasons for licensing laws is to help identify all the lost and stolen bicycles, so that if a bike is stolen, the police will know that it is yours and will be able to return it to you. It is a misdemeanor to remove or deface a serial number or identifying number on a bicycle. It is also a misdemeanor to remove or deface a license plate or registration sticker while it is current and to tamper with a locked, racked, or otherwise secured bike if you are not the owner or do not have the owner's permission.

*What equipment must I have on my bicycle?*

You must have:

**1.** A brake on at least one wheel that will allow you to make the wheel skid on dry pavement  (Minn. Stat. §169.222(6)(b))

**2.** A seat for each rider  (Minn. Stat. §169.222(2))

**3.** A red reflector on the rear  (Minn. Stat. §169.222(6)-(7))

**4.** If the bike is ridden at night, a white light on the front that can be seen 500 feet away  (Minn. Stat. §169.222(6)(a))

*Where can I ride a bicycle?*

You can ride on any roads other than freeways. (Minn. Stat. §169.305(1)(c)) If you do drive on the road, you must ride as close to the right side of the road as possible. This is with the automobile traffic, not against it. On roadways, you cannot ride more than two abreast. (Minn. Stat. §169.222(4)) You can ride on the sidewalk, except in a business district. But if you do, you must yield the right-of-way to pedestrians and you must make a sound that the pedestrian can hear before you overtake or pass that person. (Minn. Stat. §169.222(4)) If there is a bicycle path that you can use, you must ride on it instead of on the sidewalk or in the road.

*What other laws should I know about when I ride a bike?*

**1.** You must ride astride the seat of the bicycle while driving it.

**2.** You must not carry any more riders than the bike is equipped to carry (for example, no riders on handlebars or fenders).

**3.** You may not hitch a ride behind an automobile or other vehicle.

**4.** You may not carry anything that prevents you from keeping at least one hand on the handlebars.

**5.** You must park so as not to block the normal pedestrian or traffic movement.  (Minn. Stat. §169.222(5))

*Can I get a ticket if I violate these rules?*

Yes.  You can get a ticket for any violation of the traffic laws, whether you are driving an automobile, walking, or riding a bike.

## SNOWMOBILES

*Does my snowmobile have to be registered?*

Yes.  Application for registration shall be made to the commissioner of Public Safety or the commissioner of Natural Resources.  Also, no person under eighteen may register a snowmobile.  (Minn. Stat. §84.82(8))

*Where may I operate my snowmobile?*

You may not operate your snowmobile on any roadway in Minnesota, including the shoulder or county highway.  However, you may cross a roadway, provided you come to a complete stop.  (Minn. Stat. §84.87)

*Are there any other regulations I should know about?*

Yes.  It is unlawful to drive at a speed that is greater than reasonable and proper under prevailing circumstances.  This is much like the basic speed law as it applies to automobiles and motorcycles.  It is also unlawful to drive a snowmobile under the influence of drugs or alcohol, to drive a snowmobile without a headlight and taillight when circumstances require it, and to drive a snowmobile in a tree nursery.

## EMPLOYMENT AND WAGES

<table>
<tr><td>

**WHAT
DO
YOU
THINK?**

———

What are the rules for employment of persons under fourteen?  Between fourteen and sixteen?  Between sixteen and eighteen?  Over eighteen?

</td><td>

*How old do I have to be to get a job?*

There is no absolute minimum age limit for getting a job.  Generally no minors under fourteen can be permitted employment with certain exceptions (for example, corn detassling;  working as an actor, model or performer; delivering newspapers; or babysitting).  Further, no person may hire a child under sixteen to work at any job while public schools are in session.  In other words, anyone under sixteen is limited to summer jobs or jobs with restricted hours. (Minn. Stat. §181A.04)

*Can older teenagers have any job they want?*

There are restrictions and rules about the times you can work, the types of jobs you can hold, and the total hours you can work.  The rules vary, depending on your age and sex.

</td></tr>
</table>

*Part-time jobs should not interfere with high school hours.*

### Can I work during school hours?

If you are between fourteen and sixteen, you cannot have a job during school hours unless you meet a number of strict requirements. These rules are established because everyone under sixteen is supposed to attend school; the law is set up to prevent a job from interfering with school. If you are between fourteen and sixteen, in order to have a job, certain requirements must be met. Your employer must obtain an employment certificate for you and keep it available to the authorities at all times. A certificate is issued only in rare circumstances by the superintendent of schools or the head of the local board of education. Before your employer will be issued an employment certificate, the superintendent or head will look over your school records, your birth records, and will meet with you to be certain that you are over fourteen. You are also required to have a certificate from a doctor stating that you are in good health and able to do the work you plan to do. In addition, the certificate will not be issued unless you have completed all the studies taught in the schools of the school district and can read and write simple sentences correctly. (Minn. Stat. §181A.05)

*If I am under sixteen, is there any way I can work during the school year without getting an employment certificate?*

If you are under sixteen, you can work during the summer, in the evening, or on weekends during the school year. But there are restrictions on the hours you can work. No one under sixteen can be employed for more than forty hours in one week or more than eight hours in one day. Also, you cannot start work before 7:00 A.M. or stay later than 9:30 P.M. (Minn. Stat. §181A.05)

*Are there some kinds of jobs that I can't get at all simply because I'm a minor?*

Yes. The jobs you can hold differ according to your age and your sex. In general no one under eighteen may work:

1. In any place where drinks are sold for consumption on the premises, except as a musician, or as a dishwasher or busperson in a restaurant or motel that serves food as well as alcoholic drinks  (Minn. Stat. §340.14(2))

2. In any job dangerous to life, health, or morals  (Minn. Stat. §181A.09)

3. As a hired driver of a passenger-carrying vehicle  (Minn. Stat. §171.322)

*Can the person who hires me for one of these jobs get in trouble?*

Yes. It is a misdemeanor for anyone to hire a minor in violation of these rules. (Minn. Stat. §181A.12)

*What is the minimum wage?*

Both the federal and state government establish minimum wages. The federal minimum wage is $3.35 an hour as of December 31, 1980. The state minimum wage is $2.90 per hour. For teen-agers, the state minimum wage is less than $2.90 per hour because the Minnesota commissioner of Labor and Industry is required to set special rules for people under eighteen. This minimum wage rate cannot be more than 90 percent of the rate for adults, so it is now set at $2.61 per hour. (Minn. Stat. §177.24) If you have a job as a salesperson or a job where you receive tips, the minimum wage does not apply. There are complicated rules about how much you can get. (Minn. Stat. §177.28(3), (4)) In addition, if an adult is employed for a work week that is longer than forty hours, they are entitled to one and a half times the regular rate they receive. For those between sixteen and eighteen, you would be entitled to a rate at least equal to one and a half times the special minimum wage rate set by the commissioner for those under eighteen. However, no one under sixteen can be employed for more than forty hours a week.

*Must I be paid the minimum wage?*

Yes. All wage orders of the Minnesota Minimum Wage Commission apply to anyone eighteen and older. (Minn. Stat. §177.24)

*What happens if the employer doesn't pay me my wages?*

If your employer fails to pay you your wages within twenty-four hours after they are due and after you request it, you can collect an extra day's wage for each day that he or she fails to pay you. (Minn. Stat. §181.11 and .13) The law also sets up special rules for deciding how much the employer owes you if you disagree over the amount of wages the employer owes you. (Minn. Stat. §181.14)

## GUNS AND WEAPONS

*What is a dangerous weapon?*

The law says that a dangerous weapon is any firearm (gun) or anything else that is made to hurt people or used to hurt people and that could kill or seriously injure someone. (Minn. Stat. §609.02(6))

*Is it O.K. to scare people with a gun?*

No. It is a misdemeanor to point a gun at another person on purpose, even if the gun is unloaded.

*Can minors own guns?*

There is no state law that says that minors cannot own guns, but it is a misdemeanor for anyone to furnish a gun or even an air gun to a minor under fourteen without the parents' consent. It is also a misdemeanor for a parent to allow a minor under fourteen to use a gun or air gun except in the presence of the parents. In any minicipality it is a misdemeanor for anyone to sell you or give you a gun, air gun, or ammunition until you are eighteen without written consent of your parents, guardian, police department, or magistrate. (Minn. Stat. §609.66) Some cities and towns have their own ordinances that say that no one under eighteen may own a gun. Minneapolis and St. Paul have rules like this. (Mpls. Ord. Code SEc. 877.020; St. Paul Leg. Code Sec. 426.01)

*Are there special laws regarding pistols?*

A 1975 law limits the use and possession of pistols in the state of Minnesota. This law states that a person under the age of eighteen cannot possess a pistol unless he or she is in the actual presence of the parent or guardian, or for the purpose of a military drill, or for purposes of instruction under a qualified instructor. The law also requires, except in particular cases, that the owner of a pistol obtain a special permit. The manufacture or sale of a pistol called a "Saturday night special," a cheap weapon frequently used in criminal activities, is forbidden. (Minn. Stat. §642.712)



"A well regulated Militia, being necessary to the security of a free state, the right of the people to keep and bear arms, shall not be infringed."——*Third Amendment, U.S. Constitution*

*Can I carry a gun for protection?*

Usually not, even if you can legally own a gun. State law says that it is a misdemeanor to have any dangerous weapon if you intend to use it illegally. (Minn. Stat. §609.66(5))

Many cities and towns have ordinances that say it is illegal to carry a concealed weapon. This means that you may not wear a gun, knife, or any other dangerous weapon under your coat or other clothes. Generally, you cannot carry a weapon in your car or carry it in a public place even if it is visible, unless it is a hunting gun that is unloaded and broken down. (Mpls. Ord. Code Secs. 877.020 and .030; St. Paul Leg. Code Sec. 425.01)

*Can a minor own a switchblade?*

No. It is a misdemeanor for anyone, minor or adult, to own a switchblade. (Minn. Stat. §609.66(4))

## HUNTING AND FISHING

*Do I have to have a license to fish or hunt?*

Usually you must have a license to take game, to fish, or to harvest wild rice, but there are some exceptions. You must often get different licenses to take different animals. (Minn. Stat. §98.45)

*When can I hunt or fish without a license?*

You do not need a license:

1. To kill unprotected animals, usually predators like wolves, bobcats, or lynx, or undesirable animals such as skunks. (Minn. Stat. §100.26) But it is unlawful to drive a propelled vehicle intentionally to chase, run over, or kill any unprotected animals.

2. To take fish and to trap furbearing animals, except beaver and otter, if you are under sixteen and a Minnesota resident. (Minn. Stat. §98.47)

3. To take small game (anything but deer, moose, elk, bear, or caribou) if you are under thirteen and a Minnesota resident. (Minn. Stat. §98.47)

4. To take small game on land that you or your family owns. (Minn. Stat. §98.47)

*How old do I have to be to get a hunting license?*

No hunting licenses will be issued to persons under sixteen unless they have a valid firearm safety permit. Teen-agers between twelve and sixteen must have such a permit to take small game even though they do not need a license. (Minn. Stat. §98.47)

*How do I get a certificate?*

You must take a special firearms instruction course approved by the state commissioner of Natural Resources. (Minn. Stat. §97.81) The courses are to teach safety in hunting and the safe use of firearms.

*How old do I have to be to get a certificate?*

You must be at least twelve, although you can start taking the course when you are eleven and graduate when you are twelve.  (Minn. Stat. §97.83)

*Can I hunt with a gun without a certificate?*

It is illegal for you to hunt with a gun if you are under sixteen unless your parents are with you or you have a certificate.  If you have a certificate you can hunt without your parents and use your gun if you are over fourteen. (Minn. Stat. §97.83)

*Are there any other age requirements that I should know about?*

Yes.  It is illegal for persons under fourteen to hunt unless accompanied by their parents.  (Minn. Stat. §98.47)

*What is "hunting season"?*

Hunting season is a period of time during the year when  the law allows hunters to kill certain animals.  There are different seasons for different kinds of animals.  Some seasons are very short if the animals are not very numerous. (Minn. Stat. §100.27)

*What are limits?*

Because the number of some animals is limited, hunters are allowed to take only a few.  For example, each deer hunter can take only one deer.  This allows more people to hunt and controls the number of animals that are taken. (Minn. Stat. §100.28)

*Are there any other rules I should know about?*

It is illegal to:

1.  Shoot wild animals from a car or snowmobile

2.  Hunt with a firearm or bow and arrow while intoxicated or under the influence of narcotics

3.  Hunt deer with explosive or poisonous arrows

4.  Transport a firearm (except a pistol or revolver) in a motor vehicle unless it is unloaded and completely contained in a gun case that is fully enclosed

5.  Hunt deer unless you are wearing bright red or orange on your hat and coat

**6.** Kill animals by running over them with a snowmobile or automobile

**7.** Find deer or other animals by shining your headlights or other light at them  (Minn. Stat. §100.29)

**8.** Enter another's crop or pastureland during hunting season to hunt game without permission of the owner or lessees.  This does not apply to wooded areas except tree farms.  Also, you may not cut or tear down fences, buildings, grain crops, or live trees, or kill domestic livestock.  These laws can be enforced by all law enforcement officers, not just game wardens.

*What are the penalties for violating these rules?*

Most violations are misdemeanors, but some are gross misdemeanors.  It is a gross misdemeanor to hunt with a weapon while intoxicated or to shine deer.  (Minn. Stat. §97.55)  Your hunting or fishing license is immediately revoked in most cases.  (Minn. Stat. §98.52)  The conservation officers may confiscate and sell any game or fish illegally taken and all of your equipment.  For serious offenses, such as shining deer, they may confiscate your automobile or boat.  (Minn. Stat. §97.50)

*Is there anything else that I should know?*

This is just a brief summary of the hunting and fishing laws, which are very complicated.  If you plan to hunt or fish you should first apply for a license and obtain more detailed information from the Minnesota Department of Natural Resources, the county auditor, or any authorized agent of the Department of Natural Resources.  (Minn. Stat. §98.50)


## WATERSPORTS

*Do I need a special license to drive a motorboat?*

No person under thirteen may operate a motorboat of more than twenty-four horsepower unless there is a person over eighteen in the boat.  A teen-ager over thirteen but under eighteen must obtain a watercraft operator's permit to operate such a boat without an adult present.  There is an educational course and a written test required to obtain a permit.  The permit may be revoked for certain violations of watercraft safety rules.  (Minn. Stat. §§361.055, .041 and .22)

*Are there rules for water-skiers and scuba divers?*

Yes.  It is unlawful to pull a water skier at any time between one hour after sunset and sunrise of the following day.  (Minn. Stat. §361.09)(2))  Any person using artificial breathing equipment in the water is required to display a diver's flag at least thirty inches above the surface of the water.  (Minn. Stat. §361.085)

## MOVIES AND PUBLICATIONS

*Is it illegal for me to go to an X-rated movie if I'm under eighteen?*

No. But if you are under eighteen, it is illegal for the theater to sell you a ticket to any movie that "depicts nudity, sexual conduct, or sadomasochistic abuse and is harmful to minors." (Minn. Stat. §§617.292 and .294) This is a much stricter rule than the obscenity rules that limit the movies and books that may be sold to adults; it probably includes most X-rated movies and some R-rated movies.

Since the theater owner could be convicted of a gross misdemeanor, and since the owner could defend a criminal charge by showing that the motion picture rating system was complied with, most owners carefully check identification to be sure that persons admitted to R- and X-rated movies are old enough to get in according to the rating code. (Minn. Stat. §§617.296 and .297)

*Can I buy Playboy or Playgirl?*

It is not a crime for you to buy these magazines, but it may be a gross misdemeanor for someone to sell it to you. The standard for magazines is the same as for movies: it is illegal to sell books or magazines to persons under eighteen if they "depict nudity, sexual conduct, or sadomasochistic abuse and are harmful to minors." (Minn. Stat. §617.293) *Playboy* and similar magazines may fit within this definition.

## POOL HALLS, GAMBLING, AND PUBLIC DANCES

*Is it illegal for me to play pool in a pool hall?*

No. In the past it was illegal for persons under eighteen to enter a pool hall unless accompanied by their parents, but that law was repealed in 1963, and it is now legal to play pool in pool halls. (former Minn. Stat.§§617.61, .62 and .63)

*Is it illegal for minors to gamble?*

Yes. It is also illegal for adults to gamble. (Minn. Stat. §§609.75, .755 and .76)

*Is it illegal for minors to play pinball machines?*

No. It is legal to play pinball machines if no awards or prizes other than replays are given for successful playing. If there are other prizes, the pinball machine would be a gambling device and it would be illegal for both minors and adults to play it. (*McNeice v. City of Minneapolis*, 250 Minn. 142, 84 N.W.2d 232 (1957))

*Is it legal for me to go to public dances?*

No teen-ager under sixteen can attend a public dance unless accompanied by a parent, and teen-agers over sixteen and under eighteen may attend only with the written consent of their parents. (Minn. Stat. §624.49) This law does not apply to school dances, church dances, or private parties. It only applies to a dance where admission is charged and where the general public may attend. (Minn. Stat. §624.42)


## CURFEW

*What is a curfew?*

A curfew is a rule that says that people may not be on the street or in public places after a certain time of night. Usually, it is a law or ordinance requiring teen-agers to be home late at night, but if there is a riot or other civil disturbance, the authorities sometimes set a curfew for all people. Parents and dormitories often require young people to return at a certain time, and this may be called a curfew too, even though it is not a law.

*Does Minnesota have a curfew law for teen-agers?*

No. There is no state law setting a curfew, but many cities have curfew ordinances.

*What do these ordinances say?*

The St. Paul and Minneapolis ordinances are probably a lot like all of the others, although the details may be different in your city. The St. Paul ordinance applies to all teen-agers under sixteen and says that you may not "loiter, idle, wander, stroll or play" in the streets or other public places after 10:00 P.M. or before 5:00 A.M. It also says that it is illegal for your parents to allow you to do these things. (St. Paul Leg. Code §§460.01 and .02) The Minneapolis ordinance says that teen-agers under sixteen cannot "loaf, loiter, or idle" in public places after 9:30 P.M. or before 5:00 A.M. For teenagers between sixteen and eighteen the hours are 12:01 A.M. and 5:00 A.M. It also says that parents may not knowingly or carelessly allow their children to stay out after curfew. The statute says that no place of business may let you stay if you are violating curfew, and that if you refuse to leave they must call the police. (Mpls. Ord. Code §§878.020, .030, .040 and .050)

*What if I have a good reason to be out after curfew?*

Curfews are designed to keep teen-agers from "hanging around" and not to prevent them from doing things that they really need to do. That is why they use words like "loafing" and "idling." Neither of the ordinances applies if you are with an adult. (St. Paul Leg. Code §460.01; Mpls. Ord. Code §878.030) The St. Paul ordinance also makes an exception if you are on an errand for your parents, if you are working, or if there is an emergency. (St. Paul Leg. Code §460.01)

## FIREWORKS

*Is it illegal to shoot off fireworks?*

Yes. It is illegal for anyone to sell, use, or explode any fireworks. (Minn. Stat. §624.21) Cap pistols are not considered fireworks, but small firecrackers, cherry bombs, and sparklers are included. (Minn. Stat. §624.20) Naturally, public displays are allowed; these rules only apply to the unauthorized use of fireworks. (Minn. Stat. §624.22) If you violate this law you can be convicted of a misdemeanor and the police or fire marshal may seize the fireworks. (Minn. Stat. §§624.24 and 26)

## DOGS

*Do I have to have a license for my dog?*

This depends upon where you live. State law does not require you to license your dog, but state law allows counties to pass ordinances that require licenses. These ordinances usually only apply to rural areas, and the fees for licenses are kept in a fund to pay for farm animals injured or killed by dogs in the county. (Minn. Stat. §§347.08 and .21) County ordinances apply outside municipal limits only, if the municipality regulates dogs. (Minn. Stat. §347.08(1))

Minnesotans own an estimated 733,150 pets. In the Twin Cities alone, 25,428 dogs were either picked up as strays or turned in as unwanted in 1979.

*Does this mean I don't need to get a license if I live in the city?*

No. Most municipalities require you to obtain a license for your dog. Both Minneapolis and St. Paul require you to buy a license for your dog and to renew it each year. You will receive a metal tag that your dog must wear on its collar at all times. (Mpls. Ord. Code §§810.010, .030 and .070; St. Paul Leg. Code §§329.02, .03 and .07)

*Can I take my dog out for a walk without a leash?*

Again, state law does not require that dogs be leashed, but some of the larger cities, including St. Paul and Minneapolis, have ordinances that do require it. Both St. Paul and Minneapolis have ordinances that say that all dogs must be on a leash if not in a fenced area. The Minneapolis ordinance also requires the owner to clean up and dispose of solid wastes left behind by the dog when it is out on its leash. (Mpls. Ord. Code §810.80; St. Paul Leg. Code §329.08)

*What happens if I don't have a leash or license for my dog?*

In Minneapolis and St. Paul the dog license inspector (dog catcher) will seize the dog and put it in the dog pound. To get the dog back you must pay $7.50 for a pound fee plus an additional $1.00 per day for the dog's room and board, and $3.00 for a license if the dog is unlicensed. If you do not reclaim the dog within five days, it will be killed. (St. Paul Leg. Code §§329.09-.10, .13 and .15; Mpls. Ord. Code §§810.020, .130 and .150-.170)

*Larger cities require that dogs be leashed when not fenced in.*

*Is there a limit on the number of dogs I can own?*

Again, there is nothing in state law.  There is, however, a Minneapolis ordinance that says that you must have a permit from the Minneapolis commissioner of Health to keep more than three dogs. (Mpls. Ord. Code §810.230)

*Can I get in trouble if my dog bites someone?*

Yes.  If your dog attacks a person in any place where that person has a right to be, you can be sued and made to pay for the damages the dog caused.  This is true even though you were not careless and did not know that the dog might bite a person;  the law says you are strictly liable.  (For the consequences of this liability, see Chapter 1 on civil law.)  (Minn. Stat. §347.22)


## LITTERING

*Is it illegal to litter?*

Yes.  It is a misdemeanor to dump or throw any kind of trash, garbage, or harmful or dangerous thing on the streets or highways, or on private or public land along the road without the owner's consent.  If you accidentally drop any litter on the highway, you are required to clean it up.  The second littering offense (and any additional offenses after that) carries a minimum fine of $100. The judge may order a person convicted of littering either to go to jail or to pick up litter along the highways for four to eight hours. (Minn. Stat. §§169.42 and .91)

## PROBLEM 1

Michael, a fourteen-year-old, wishes to work at McDonalds. He hopes to save the money he makes for a car. He intends to buy the car when he is fifteen and apply for a restricted license.

1. Can Michael work at McDonalds? If so, under what restrictions?

2. Can he buy a car at age fifteen?

3. Will he qualify for a restricted license?

4. What do you think of a person Michael's age working?

5. What do you think about his intent to buy a car at age fifteen?

6. What factors should Michael consider—both pro and con?

## PROBLEM 2

Donnie is a fifteen-year-old high school sophomore. He had worked full-time in the greenhouse at Jackson's Nursery during Christmas vacation, and as soon as the spring gardening season began, Mr. Jackson rehired him as temporary help. Donnie was soon working in the nursery's retail store from 3:00 P.M. to 10:00 P.M. on weeknights (which necessitated his "slipping away" from school a little early some days), 6:30 A.M. to 6:00 P.M. on Saturday, and 10:00 A.M. to 6:00 P.M. on Sundays.

A lawyer friend of Mr. Jackson, who also is a neighbor of Donnie's family, suggests to Mr. Jackson that he may not be employing Donnie in a legal manner. The spring gardening season being nearly over, Mr. Jackson fires Donnie.

Donnie waits three weeks for his last paycheck, which never comes through the mail. Donnie calls the nursery and is finally told by Mr. Jackson himself that because his employment was illegal, the nursery does not have to pay him. Donnie still does not have his check.

1. Was Donnie's work during the Christmas holiday legal?

2. Does Donnie need an employment certificate to work?

3. What rules has Donnie's employment at Jackson's Nursery violated?

4 Can Mr. Jackson be penalized for violating these rules if he knows Donnie's age? If he doesn't know? How do you think this violation should be handled?

5. Is Donnie entitled to his last two weeks of pay? Can Mr. Jackson be compelled to pay Donnie's wages? What can Donnie do to ensure that he will receive his earnings?

# HOW TO ENFORCE THE LAW

You have had a quick view of your legal rights and responsibilities, but how do you enforce these rights? Sometimes informal pressures—such as the desire to secure the good opinion of fellow citizens—will bring about compliance. However, sometimes there is a dispute as to what a person's legal rights and responsibilities are, and citizens must resort to the courts to settle the matter.

Courts have two distinct functions: (a) to determine the facts in disputed situations, and (b) to determine the law applicable to the facts. Juries are frequently used to determine facts, but judges determine the law that is applicable. In some cases there is no jury; then the judge will also determine the facts. Usually, there must be some dispute before a lawsuit is brought, though there are some proceedings in which there is no immediate controversy but which are brought in a court to be sure the rights of all affected parties are protected.

## JURY TRIAL

The Constitutions of the United States and the state of Minnesota guarantee every person accused of a crime a trial by jury. A jury is selected from the qualified voters in the district, and the usual number on a jury is twelve. The jury hears the evidence and, if testimony is in conflict, must decide which testimony is to be believed. (see the Sixth Amendment to the U.S. Constitution, and the Minnesota Constitution, Art. I, §§4 and 6)

We have seen that most court cases are civil rather than criminal. Is a person entitled to a jury in every civil case? The Seventh Amendment to the U.S. Constitution states, "In suits at common law, where the value in controversy shall exceed twenty dollars the right of trial by jury shall be preserved, and no fact tried by a jury, shall be otherwise re-examined in any Court of the United States, then according to the rules of common law." Article 1, Section 4 of the Minnesota Constitution says, "The right of trial by jury shall remain inviolate, and shall extend to all cases at law without regard to the amount in controversy, but a jury trial may be waived by the parties in all cases in the manner prescribed by law; and the legislature may provide that the agreement of five-sixths of any jury in any civil action or proceeding, after not less than six (6) hours' deliberation, shall be a sufficient verdict therein." You will notice the reference to "cases at law" here, and the federal Constitution's reference to "suits at common law." These phrases refer to the types of case that were regarded as common law cases at the time the Constitution was adopted and are especially distinguished from cases in equity.

What is *equity*? It is a system emphasizing justice and fairness rather than mere reference to specific rules or statutes. There are several equitable principles that have come down to us: "Equity looks upon that as done which ought to have been done;" "Equity suffers not a right without a remedy;" "Equity follows the law." Perhaps an example might help to define equity. If A buys merchandise from B and agrees to pay $100 for the merchandise but fails to make the payment when it is due and refuses to pay, B may bring a legal action to collect the $100 due on the contract. B might demand that a jury determine whether the full amount is owed or whether A actually did make the promise to pay for the goods. This would be an action "at law." However, if A encroaches on B's property by tearing down a fence and using part of B's property for a driveway, B may want A to stop the encroachment instead of wanting damage for the property taken. B would then ask a court to enjoin A from further interference with B's property as well as damages for the unwarranted interference, and B's seeking this injunction would be an equitable action. Frequently there are elements of both law and equity in one case. If there is an adequate remedy at law, an action in equity is not available.

The British legal system, from which our American system evolved, has separate judges in law and equity. Equity matters were formerly called chancery matters, because the chancellor, one of the King's advisors, decided these cases. Courts of equity or chancery sprang from the authority of the church and were designed to appeal to the conscience. In America, the same courts were authorized to try cases in law and equity, but the rules governing the two types were different. Juries were never used in equitable matters. You can see that much of the distinction between law and equity is historical, but this history determines whether or not there is a right to a jury trial. The distinction is mentioned because despite the constitutional provisions, not all civil suits require jury trials.

Jurors for state courts may be selected from qualified voters of the county or district in which they serve, and the same list may be used by both the district, county, or municipal courts in the large counties. Examination of jurors is conducted by the court or by the respective attorneys for the parties to a lawsuit before the court at the start of a trial, and if it appears a juror is closely connected with one of the parties or is prejudiced, that juror may be challenged (removed from the jury panel) for cause. The attorneys for each litigant also have a limited number of *peremptory* challenges, (challenges precluding further debate or action, which may be used to strike from the panel prospective jurors the attorney does not want without giving any reason for not wanting that panel member.

If the question is solely one of interpretation of the law, a jury is not chosen—the solution of such problems is the duty of the judge. Also, two parties to a lawsuit may agree on a statement of fact but ask the court to determine the consequences, and sometimes even if there is a dispute as to facts, the parties leave the fact finding to the judge.

## ADMINISTRATIVE TRIBUNALS

Statutes setting up new rights and duties have sometimes set up administrative tribunals to hear and decide the facts; these usually concern rights that do not exist in common law. In such cases a trial by jury is not available. An example is worker's compensation—a system of law enacted by the legislature that provides certain specific payments to employees injured in the performance of their duties or while at the place of employment, regardless of fault or assumed risk that could be otherwise attributed to the employee. The payment is made to the employee if he or she is injured, or to specified dependents if the employee is killed in such an accident. The law sets up a schedule of payments, and the compensation judges (appointed officers) hear disputed cases to determine if the injury or death arose out of the injured party's employment and the extent of the injury or disability. Appeals from the compensation judge are heard by an appointed three-member worker's compensation board of appeals. An appeal from this court is taken directly to the supreme court of Minnesota. A jury is not selected at any state in the proceedings. The facts as found by the worker's compensation court of appeals are not changed unless not supported by the evidence. The court may apply the law differently to the same facts and must state reasons for so doing.

Direct appeals to the supreme court are also taken from such administrative tribunals as the tax court of Minnesota, the Department of Economic Security, and the Department of Commerce, among others. Decisions of the Department of Human Rights, which deals with charges of racial or sexual discrimination, may be appealed to the district court. In none of these proceedings is there a jury. Usually the facts as found by the first tribunal are given the weight that would be given to a finding of fact by a jury if there is some evidence to support the finding, even though reasonable people might come to a different conclusion based on the same evidence. Basically, the philosophy is that the trier of fact, observing the witnesses, is in a better position to decide between conflicting witnesses, or to decide the weight of the evidence, than is a court reviewing its decision, unless the record simply does not provide a basis for the decision.

## THE MINNESOTA COURT SYSTEM

Having mentioned tribunals which are not part of the regular court system, let us proceed to an outline of the Minnesota court system. Minnesota has a supreme court established by the state constitution, a district court, and a system of county courts. In most counties of the state the county court serves more than one county, but there is a clerk of court in each county. Hennepin and Ramsey Counties have municipal courts whose jurisdiction extends to the entire county, each having several municipal judges. Dakota and Anoka Counties each have five county judges. The tri-county district of Stearns, Sherburne, and Benton has five judges. Hennepin and Ramsey Counties have separate probate courts to handle the administration of deceased persons' estates, guardianships, and incompetency proceedings.

All state judges in Minnesota—from the supreme court judges to the judges of county, municipal, or probate courts—are subject to election for terms set by statute. To be eligible to run for election, the candidate must be "learned in the law," which has been interpreted to mean a person admitted to practice law in Minnesota and not under suspension or disbarment. District court judges must be residents of the district in which they are to serve, and county judges of the county-district in which they will serve, even though the chief justice may temporarily make assignments to help in other districts.

### County Courts

In the eighty-five counties that operate under the county court districts, the county court has power to try cases in actions at law in which the amount in controversy does not exceed $5,000 (except for cases involving title to real estate), misdemeanors, ordinance violations, preliminary hearings on other criminal offenses committed within the county, and juvenile proceedings, as well as handling the administration of estates of deceased persons, guardianships, and incompetency proceedings.

These county courts also handle forcible entry and unlawful detainer matters involving land within the county. This type of action is used by a landlord who wants to evict a tenant. He charges the tenant with "unlawfully detaining" the property; the tenant is served with notice of the hearing and is given a chance to appear in court. There the landlord presents evidence (for example, nonpayment of rent or failure to observe a notice terminating the tenancy). If the tenant is guilty, the court orders that person's removal and sets a date for such removal. If the tenant disproves the allegation (as by producing a receipt for the claimed rent due, or by proving the notice terminating his or her tenancy was inadequate, the court denies the plea for the tenant's removal.

These county courts may also hear proceedings relating to trusts, divorce or separate maintenance, adoption or change of name, the reciprocal enforcement of support act, and quiet title to real estate or mortgage foreclosures "by action."

In Ramsey County the St. Paul Municipal Court tries matters when the amount in controversy does not exceed $6,000. It may not entertain actions asking for equitable relief, divorce, or issue certain writs. The jurisdiction of the Municipal Court of Hennepin County is also limited to cases where the amount in controversy does not exceed $6,000. These municipal courts may also entertain actions relating to forcible entry or unlawful detainer, try persons accused of minor crimes and ordinance violations, and hold preliminary hearings in other cases. The jurisdiction of the municipal courts in Hennepin and Ramsey Counties extends to all of the county.

Each county court or municipal court tries cases arising in the county or counties where the court is located, and all of them are "courts of record." If appeals are taken, those appeals are based on the written record.


## District Courts

The District Court of Minnesota is defined as being one court, though there are ten judicial districts. Judges of the district court must be residents of the districts where they preside at the time they are elected and during their terms of office. The legislature may alter the number of judges or the boundaries of judicial districts, but the office of a district judge may not be abolished during his or her term of office. There must be at least two district judges in each district. District courts have original jurisdiction in almost all civil and criminal cases except probate matters (such as estates and guardianships). A district judge may be assigned to a district other than the one in which he or she was elected when the chief justice of the state supreme court determines a need for the judge's services exists in another district so the work of the various districts may be more equally distributed. District courts may take both legal and equitable matters and are not limited by dollar amounts in their jurisdictions. Also, any district judge may be assigned to assist the supreme court for a temporary period. Even though the county court or municipal court might have the power to try a case, the case might be brought in district court because these courts have concurrent jurisdiction over many of the matters that the county or municipal courts could try. Except in Hennepin County, a district court may hear appeals from conviction of a municipal ordinance. If such a conviction is appealed, and the appellant did not have a jury trial in the first court, that person may demand a jury in the district court and get a complete new trial. The district court does not hear appeals from county or municipal courts in civil cases, but certain appeals from the probate courts to the district court are provided.

In some districts there is some specialization of duties. In the Second Judicial District of Ramsey County, one district judge is designated as a family court judge to handle divorce and related matters, and that judge may have assistants. In the Fourth Judicial District of Hennepin County, one district court judge is designated a family court judge by the chief judge of the district with the approval of a majority of the judges of the district. Also, in Hennepin and Ramsey Counties, a district judge handles juvenile court matters—one in each district. In the less populous counties, the county courts would handle both family court and juvenile matters.

### The Supreme Court

The supreme court of Minnesota is the state's highest court. It is composed of a chief justice and not less than six, nor more than eight, associate justices. At present, the court has the full number of justices authorized. The supreme court is primarily an appellate court, hearing appeals from district courts and from the various administrative tribunals established by statute. There is no jury trial in the supreme court; facts are accepted as found by the lower court or administrative tribunal in most cases; and since the jury's function is the finding of fact, this is a function that is not present in the supreme court. This court also may make rules regarding the conduct and disciplining of attorneys, including suspension from practice or disbarmnt. It also determines rules of pleading and procedure (the process of bringing and trying court actions) for all the courts in the state. Other courts may adopt rules for their own conduct not in conflict with the supreme court rules. As an example, the supreme court may decide the form a complaint (a document stating the grounds for the court action) should take, but the judges in a particular district might specify that the pleading be flat and unfolded with no cover, while another district may want it covered with a folder and folded. Also, within certain limits set by legislation, the courts determine their own times of meeting and their calendars (the order in which cases will be heard).

### Conciliation Court

Because a successful lawsuit is best tried by people who know what court is appropriate for the matter involved and the technical rules of procedure, as well as applicable law, the matter of conducting trials or lawsuits is reserved to attorneys admitted and licensed to practice by the Minnesota Supreme Court. An exception to this rule is the right of any person to represent himself or herself without counsel if he or she so wishes. There is also an exception in divisions of the municipal court or county court, which are called conciliation courts. In such courts, one municipal or county judge hears the participants in a less formal setting than in the ordinary court case. Sometimes lawyer-referees are used to hear cases. Usually the complainant states the complaint to the clerk of the court, who sends a copy of the complaint by mail to the opposing party, who must be a resident of that county, and sets a date for trial. At the appointed time each party appears and gives the judge his or her version of the controversy with any written or other evidence in his or her possession, and the judge decides the controversy. Neither party in these conciliation courts is required to have an attorney. There are no formal pleadings. Relief is limited to recovery of money, and the amounts in controversy may not exceed $1,000. There is no jury in a conciliation court. Either party may appeal a conciliation court judgment to the regular municipal or county court; then the filing fees, pleadings, representation by attorneys, and the like are the same as in any other case.

If there is a vacancy in any of the state courts, the governor fills the vacancy until the general election occurring more than one year after the date of appointment, when the appointee is subject to election.

## APPEALS

If you are a party to a lawsuit and lose, what can you do? Of course you can accept the judgment as rendered. Some cases may be appealed to a higher court, because the law applied is thought to be in conflict with either the Minnesota or U.S. Constitution or with previous decisions of the Minnesota U.S. Supreme Court. When the U.S. Supreme Court has ruled on a matter, the state courts must follow that decision. This is partly so the administration of justice will be uniform, and partly so that ordinary citizens may plan their affairs with some degree of certainty as to the results. The theory behind this practice is that if the Supreme Court is in error, the people, through the legislature or by constitutional amendment if it is a constitutional question, may change the effect of the decision. Usually a court will not reverse its own decision or overrule an earlier decision.

An appeal may be taken: if the judge in the trial court gave erroneous instructions to the jury; if the judge permitted evidence that should not have been permitted; if an attorney referred to facts that had not been placed in evidence; or if there is no evidence in the record to support the verdict or judgment. Sometimes the original decision is reversed; sometimes the matter is remanded (sent back) to the lower court for more evidence on a specific point; and sometimes the appellant, whose motion for a new trial may have been denied, gets a new trial. However, there must be some reason that is considered by the law to be a reason for appeal—not simply the disappointment of the losing party. Also, any appeal must be filed within specified times and in proper form.

Once a lawsuit has been finally decided, the parties cannot bring the same matter into court again—that is, a party who loses the case cannot file a new suit hoping that a new jury might give a different result in the same set of circumstances.

## ARBITRATION

We have alluded to triers of fact other than juries, such as administrative tribunals. It is also possible that two parties to a dispute might agree to submit the question in dispute to an arbitrator. The statutes provide that where two parties have agreed to submit a dispute to arbitration, the arbitrator's award (decision) will be enforced by the courts, unless there is fraud on the part of the arbitrator, or the arbitrator exceeded the authority given by the agreement of the parties. If two parties agree to arbitrate a dispute in certain circumstances and then one party refuses to proceed to select an arbitrator, the court will select the arbitrator. (Minn. Stat. §572.10)

## FEDERAL COURTS

We should not ignore federal courts in a discussion of Minnesota law. The United States has federal district courts, circuit courts of appeals, and the United States Supreme Court, as well as specialized courts such as the federal court of claims and the federal tax court. Access to federal courts is somewhat more restricted than access to state courts in ordinary civil matters. For example, in suits between citizens of different states, the Constitution provides that the federal courts have jurisdiction, but the amount in controversy must exceed $10,000 before such a case can be brought into federal district court. This does not leave the parties without recourse. The moving party, usually called the plaintiff, can sue in the courts of the state where the defendant is found if adequate service (notice of court action) is made on the opposing party; then the state court may be used to enforce the claim. If the claim is for a sum of money arising out of a contract made in Minnesota that was also to have been performed in the state, then Minnesota law is applied by the state court trying the suit. Similarly, you might use Minnesota courts to enforce rights granted under federal law. Suppose you are employed in an industry subject to the federal wage-hour law for less than that law specifies in wages. That wage-hour law gives an underpaid employee the right to sue the employer for the underpayment for up to two years previous and, in addition, an equal amount as damages for the underpayment. You can sue such an employer in the Minnesota state courts for this double payment of the amount due under federal law, and the state courts then will be enforcing federal law.

It is a fundamental principle that the state of Minnesota or the United States government cannot be sued without their consent. The U.S. Court of Claims was set up to handle suits against the United States under laws passed by Congress specifying when suits against the United States might be brought. Minnesota has a State Claims Commission—a body of legislators, three from each house—with the authority to hear claims against the state that cannot be brought in the courts. If the claim is small ($250 or less), the commission may decide the claim should be paid; and if funds are available in the budget of the department from whose funds it should be paid, the claim is settled. In the case of larger claims or where no funds are available, the commission makes recommendations to the legislature, and then the legislature appropriates money for any approved claims.

# DUE PROCESS AND EQUAL PROTECTION

*The Student Lawyer* is not intended to be a comprehensive look at the entire body of law. We have attempted to place laws in the book that would be of interest to students. We may have left some out; we may have included some that may not affect you. Nevertheless, the concept behind *The Student Lawyer* is based on a paraphrase of a famous expression: law is too important to be left to the lawyer. The law is every citizen's responsibility. Each citizen, no matter what sex, age, national origin, or experience, must know something about the law. Society cannot function with an uneducated populace.

In light of this concept this appendix will deal with two key rights extended to all citizens and found in the Fourteenth Amendment to the United States Constitution, "due process of law" and "equal protection of the law." The amendment states:

> All persons born or naturalized in the United States, and subject to the jurisdiction thereof, are citizens of the United States and of the state wherein they reside. No State shall make or enforce any law which shall abridge the privileges or immunities of citizens of the United States; nor shall any State deprive any person of life, liberty, or property, without due process of law; nor deny to any person within its jurisdiction the equal protection of the laws.

## DUE PROCESS OF LAW

What does due process of law mean? This question can be illustrated with another question. Is it really fair that the authorities can legally take my old jalopy, which has been parked in front of my house on a city street for more than two days, auction it off, and keep the money without notifying me? The concept of due process involves the idea of "fair play." Due process is essentially a question of fundamental fairness. In examining fundamental fairness, two areas must be discussed: one regarding the *substance* of the law, the other regarding the *procedure* by which the law is carried out. Is the law itself fair? Is the procedure by which the law is carried out also fair? The Fourteenth Amendment forbids a state to deny any person within that state life, liberty, or property without due process of law. In other words, no person can be denied any of these three basic individual rights without some sort of fair system of rules and procedures.

A look at the historical development of the right to counsel should provide some insight into the fundamental fairness concept of due process. In the past, the Fourteenth Amendment meant that as long as the state provided fundamentally fair laws, enforced them in a fundamentally fair way, and set up fair procedures, a person's life, liberty, or property could be taken away after that person went through the process of a trial. For example, a woman was charged with the crime of "theft under $100." She could not afford an attorney to represent her. As long as she was granted a fundamentally fair trial in which she was afforded her full trial rights, due process of law would not be violated if she was found guilty, even though no attorney assisted her during the proceedings. It was formerly presumed by the Supreme Court that the judge would guard the defendant's rights and the offense was a minor one anyway. This rationale was felt to be reasonable and also necessitated by the prohibitive costs of providing an attorney to every person charged with a crime.

In addition to the above considerations, many state courts felt that the Fifth Amendment to the United States Constitution, which also embodied the due process concept, dealt only with the federal courts. The United States Supreme Court itself felt that the first ten amendments (known as the Bill of Rights) dealt only with the federal judiciary and that Fourteenth Amendment due process did not apply Fifth Amendment due process standards to the states but was included so that the states would provide their own fundamentally fair systems of justice. Remember, the Constitution was set up to provide both a federal system and individual state systems. The Tenth Amendment, the last amendment in the Bill of Rights, states," The powers not delegated to the United States by the Constitution, nor prohibited by it to the States, are reserved to the States, respectively, or to the people." Due to this famous "states' rights" amendment, the Supreme Court felt for many years that due process under the Fourteenth Amendment, which deals with the states, meant something different from due process of law under the Fifth Amendment, which deals with the United States government. Thus, in cases other than those punishable by death, counsel was provided to poor persons charged with crime only under ' "special circumstances." There was no general rule for providing counsel.

However, the Court has reversed its position and begun to incorporate the due process of law of the Fifth Amendment into the due process of law specified in the Fourteenth Amendment. Returning to our example of the right to counsel, in 1963 the Court held that the states were required by the due process clause of the Fourteenth Amendment to furnish counsel to all poor persons charged with felonies. (*Gideon v. Wainwright*, 372 U.S. 792 (1963)) The Court has since broadened this concept to entitle a poor person to appointed counsel at trial and on appeal, when being interrogated by the police, when being viewed in a police lineup after formally charged with a crime, and at preliminary hearings on a felony charge. The right to counsel was extended to juvenile proceedings in the *Gault* case we discussed earlier, and to revocations of probation or parole in most cases.

In the latest development, the Court has extended the right to counsel implied by the Fifth and Sixth Amendments through the Fourteenth Amendment to any person charged with any offense for which he or she may be confined (jailed). In other words, no person may be jailed without having had the assistance of counsel before a plea is entered. If there is "significant likelihood" that a defendant could be jailed, he or she must have the assistance of counsel. (*Argersinger v. Hamlin*, 407 U.S. 25 (1972)) If the person cannot afford an attorney, the state must provide one.

Due process means more than the right to a lawyer's assistance. It means that in any dispute there shall be an opportunity for trial or review by some authority who is not personally affected by the outcome—in other words, an impartial trier of the facts. It also involves the idea that the law itself must conform to the limits set by the state and the federal constitutions. The law must apply equally to all persons. It must afford all persons a workable opportunity for defense against any charge made against them.

A person accused of a crime has a right to be tried before a jury of "peers." When juries are restricted to particular classes of people who may be prejudiced against the defendant, due process is violated. An accused person has the right to understand the proceedings and if he or she is deaf or does not understand the language, then an interpreter should be appointed. (Minn. Stat. §611.30)

Due process contains procedural safeguards against arbitrariness, prejudice, and bias. This is why police officers cannot arrest a person simply because they think a person doesn't look right. If police officers stop a car simply because they think the driver is acting in a "suspicious manner," they cannot justify the arrest. However, if they see a person covered with blood throwing something away which might be a weapon, and running, they might have reasonable cause to believe a felony has been committed and the person who threw the object and started to run committed it. If an officer has a reasonable belief that an immediate arrest is necessary to prevent escape, then an arrest without a warrant is justified. (*State v. Stark*, 288 Minn. 286, 179 N.W. 2d 597 (1970))

It is not due process to elicit information that may incriminate a suspect by a ruse, such as a pretense of offering help, or by detaining the suspect until he or she is willing to answer any questions the captors ask. The rule that suspects must be given a warning that they are under arrest; that they have a right to remain silent; that they have a right to an attorney's counsel; and that if they do answer questions, the answers may be used against them is a part of our due process guarantee. To be sure this rule is adhered to, evidence procured without this warninig is not admissible in court.

If an officer hears a radio report that a felony has been committed—specifically, that thieves have entered a store after hours, and it is believed they drove a car of a specific description, and immediately thereafter the officer sees a car of that description on the road—the officer is justified in stopping it. If the officer sees a pile of merchandise with price tags on them but no wrappings lying in the seat, there would be reasonable grounds for arresting the driver for theft. (Note that the police officer may stop a car if there is an actual reason for suspicion. State v. Engholm, Minn., 290 N.W. 2d 780 (1980))

A suspect who is arrested is entitled to be told why. If the officer says there is a warrant for the arrest, the suspect must be shown the warrant at the earliest opportunity. (Minn. Stat. §629.32)

Due process also includes the idea of administering justice free from passion and prejudice. If it appears that everyone in a locality has read accounts of a lurid crime for which a suspect is to be tried, the suspect may request the trial be moved to some locality where there is a greater possibility of getting an impartial jury. (Minn. Stat. §627.01) Jurors may be challenged for "implied bias" when they are related to a victim of a crime or the person accused of crime to the ninth degree, (Minn. Stat. §631.31) which is a very remote relaionship. In some closely-knit communities this might exclude many potential jurors.

Due process is also required in civil matters. A person's property may not be taken for public use without a procedure that both insures that the proposed use is a public use (not for the benefit of a private person) and that fair compensation is given.

With our emphasis on due process for a person accused of crime, what about the person who is committed to a hospital against his or her will for treatment of a mental condition? Consider the following cases:

1. An older man is physically unable to care for himself, can't bathe, can't get to a clinic, doesn't eat properly, is forgetful, fails to pay utility bills and is threatened with having them shut off, refuses to open his door to callers under the fear they may harm him, sits up nights with his television on loudly, and sleeps in the daytime. His neighbors are convinced he cannot manage his own affairs.

2. A lady has hallucinations, hears voices where there are none, calls a cab to take her to the bank on Saturday when the banks are closed, is not dressed fit to protect herself from the weather, says she must get to the bank and draw out her money because a voice tells her the bank is dishonest. You are afraid she will lose the money or be robbed of it, if she does manage to get to the bank.

What should you do? Neither of these people has threatened any harm to anyone else.

In the case of a neglected child, the juvenile court can entertain a petition in which the court declares the child dependent or neglected. What can be done for those adults who are just as helpless about taking care of themselves?

There are various degrees of interference with a person's liberty permissible under these and similar circumstances. On a showing that a person is incapable of managing his or her affairs by reason of "old age or imperfection or deterioration of mentality," a guardian may be appointed. Appointment of a guardian implies a finding of incompetence, and a person under guardianship may not vote or enter into contracts. Before the guardian is appointed, the proposed ward must have notice that a petition for guardianship is to be heard, the date of the hearing, and the place of the hearing. He or she must be given an opportunity to oppose the petition. The county court in most counties, or the probate court in Ramsey and Hennepin Counties, hears the petitioner and the proposed ward if the ward appears, decides whether a guardianship is appropriate, and whether the proposed guardian is a proper person.

Some elderly people will acknowledge that they are incapable of managing their own affairs, but they are averse to being declared incompetent. Minnesota also provides for appointment of a "conservator" for such a person, a person unable to take care of self or property, or "who because of old age or other cause is likely to be deceived or imposed upon by artful or designing person." The conservator has many of the same responsibilities as a guardian, but the person under conservatorship is not declared incompetent and can still vote.

Any person over fourteen years of age can petition for appointment of a guardian or conservator of his or her choice. If he or she does not petition for the appointment, a hearing must be held before the appointment. When the guardian or conservator is appointed, the court may require he or she give bond to protect the ward or conservatee against improper use of the assets.

Sometimes the appointment of a guardian or conservator for a person who is really not of sound mind is all that is required. In other cases there may be danger a person of unsound mind may harm other people, and a petition for commitment to a state hospital may be necessary.

If there is an emergency, a statement by a physician that the person has been examined by the physician within the last fifteen days and is in imminent danger of causing personal harm or harm to others may be sufficient authority to get that person to a hospital. (Minn. Stat. §253A.04) "A peace or health officer may take a person into custody and transport him to a licensed physician or hospital if such person has reason to believe such person is mentally ill or mentally deficient and is in imminent danger of injuring himself or others if not immediately restrained." Any person hospitalized pursuant to this section may be held for up to seventy-two hours after admission (exclusive of Saturdays, Sundays, or holidays), unless a petiiton for commitment of such person has been filed in the probate court. If the head of the hospital deems a discharge not be in the best interests of the person, the family, or the public, and no other petiiton has been filed, the administrator shall, prior to the expiration of the seventy-two hours, file a petition for commitment of such person. Upon filing the petition, the court may order the detention of the person until determination of the matter. (Minn. Stat. §253.A.07)

After the filing of the petition, the court shall appoint two examiners, at least one of whom shall be a licensed physician. Examination shall be at a hospital, a public health facility, or the home of the proposed patient. No persons are to be present during the examination unless authorized by the examiners. The court may require the examiner to file two copies of the report prior to the hearing, one copy to be available to the counsel for the proposed patient.

If the court finds the patient (1) has attempted or threatened to take his or her own life, (2) has failed to protect himself or herself from exploitation by others, (3) has failed to care for his or her own needs for food, clothing, shelter, safety, and medical care, and there is no alternative to involuntary hospitalization, the court shall commit the person to a public hospital or private institution, subject to mandatory review within sixty days. (Minn. Stat. §253A.07)

Inebriates are comitted under a similar process, except then the mandatory review takes place in forty-five days.

A federal district court has ruled that mental patients cannot be forcibly medicated except when failure to do so would result in a substantial likelihood of physical harm to the patient, other patients, or the staff. (*Rogers v. Okin*, 478 F. Supp. 1342 (1979))

A U.S. Supreme Court decision (*Vitek V. Jones*, 455 U.S. 480 (1980)) indicates that a prison inmate has a right to challenge a transfer to a mental hospital. In that decision the Court recapped the elements of due process, saying that states could not transfer prisoners to mental hospitals without: (1) written notice to the prisoner that the transfer was being contemplated; (2) a full hearing long enough after the notice to allow the prisoner to prepare for it; (3) a chance for the prisoner to present witnesses at the hearing, and to cross-examine witnesses called by the state; (4) an indepenent decision-maker to preside over the hearing; (5) a written statement to the prisoner citing evidence and reasons for the transfer; and (6) the prisoner being advised of the procedural rights.

## EQUAL PROTECTION OF THE LAW

Equal protection of the law is an almost self-defining proposition—that is, each and every citizen is guaranteed the same treatment under the law. But this leads you to an obvious question: If the Fourteenth Amendment does not permit the state to deny any person within its jurisdiction equal protection of the law, why can I as a student be treated differently from adults? This question can be asked in a more specific manner. For example, Why do I have to attend school when an adult does not? Isn't that unequal protection of the laws? We have already examined the Minnesota statute that says that every student between the ages of seven and sixteen must attend school. We have also seen that in many areas students or minors are in a different category from other people. How can this be done when the Fourteenth Amendment seems to prohibit classification of people? Isn't classification of people in fact unequal protection of the laws?

The U.S. Supreme Court has addressed itself to this question on many occasions. The Court has said that classification of people is not necessarily unequal protection of the laws. Rather, as long as the classification is reasonable—that is, the law that the state has passed classifies people on a reasonable and rational basis—such a law is constitutional. However, the Court has set up a further test beyond the reasonable test. The Court has said that: (a) when the state starts to deal with a fundamental interest of the person (for example, freedom of expression), or (b) when the state attempts to classify based on a suspect classification (for example, by race), the state must show a compelling interest in classifying in this manner, or such a law will be presumed to be unconstitutional because it denies equal protection of the laws. Compelling interests might be public health, public safety, or a serious need for uniformity of regulation.

What does the rational basis test and the compelling interest test mean to you as a student? The U.S. Supreme Court has said in the case of *San Antonio School District v. Rodriques* (411 U.S. 1 (1973)) that it is permissible for one district in a state to spend more money for the education of its students than another district in that state. So, District A may be able to spend $1,200 for each student's education, whereas District B may only be able to spend $690 on each student's education. The fact that District A is a wealthy community is irrelevant in terms of equal protction of the laws. Since the state has set up a reasonable method of obtaining tax money (in other words, property taxes), the fact that District A has a higher property tax upon which to raise the money is permissible. Such a method for financing education is reasonable, the Court felt. Therefore, even though the classification set up some degree of unfairness, such classification does not violate the Fourteenth Amendment equal protection of the law concept. However, should any state set up a classification based on race (for example, black students to attend all-black schools, white students to attend all-white schools), such a classification would be a suspect classification. At that point there is a burden on the state to show a compelling interest why such a classification has been set up. If the state is not able to do so, such a classification will be considerd a denial of equal protection of the laws to the citizens affected. Remember *Tinker v. Des Moines Independent School District* (393 U.S. 503 (1969)). Students do not shed their rights as citizens at the schoolhouse gate. If the state attempted, for example, to regulate a student's right to travel during the school year, such a classification might be considered unconstitutional since it denies the equal protection of the laws to the student in a fundamental interest—namely, the right to travel.

When dealing with classifications, every citizen must understand the differences between reasonable classifications and classifications based on a fundamental interest or suspect classifications. Sometimes these differences are very difficult to determine. When a regulation seems contrary to a citizen's fundamental interest, or when two opposing fundamental interests seem to clash, a case in controversy is set up; there are two opposing parties who take differing views as to their rights and responsibilities under the law, and the matter becomes ready for a court determination. The orderly balancing of fundamental interests, one against the other, is at the heart of the need for the Supreme Court to be the final interpreter of the supreme law of the land, the United States Constitution.

# APPENDIX C

# AGENCIES
# OF
# ASSISTANCE

It would be an impossible task for a book that is intended to be used statewide to list every local agency of assistance. If we did so, we would have a book five times the size of this one. However, there are agencies that are common to every area to provide needed services. These agencies are rich informational sources on some of the topics we have covered. Perhaps a class project that might also be a great community service would be to list these various agencies and their functions. The agencies listed below should give students a good start.

## STATE OFFICES

Senate Public Information
Room B-29, Capitol
St. Paul, MN 55155
612-296-0504

House Information
Room 8, Capitol
St. Paul, MN 55155
612-296-2146

Senate "Hotline"
612-296-8088

House "House Call"
612-296-9283

Senate Index
Room 211, Capitol
St. Paul, MN 55155
612-296-2887

House Index
Room 211, Capitol
St. Paul, MN 55155
612-296-6646

Office of the Governor
Room 130, Capitol
St. Paul, MN 55155
612-296-3391

Attorney General's Office
102 State Capitol
St. Paul, MN 55155
612-296-6196

Governor's Office of Volunteer Services
127 University Avenue
St. Paul, MN 55101
612-296-4731

MN House of Representatives
Educational Services
124D, State Capitol
St. Paul, MN 55155
612-296-8081


## STATE DEPARTMENTS


Department of Corrections
430 Metro Square Bldg.
St. Paul, MN 55101
612-296-6133

Department of Health
717 Delaware St. SE
Minneapolis, MN 55414

Department of Human Rights
200 Capitol Square Bldg.
St. Paul, MN 55101
612-296-5663

Department of Labor & Industry
5th floor, Space Center
444 Lafayette Road
St. Paul, MN 55101
612-296-6107

Department of Public Service
160 E. Kellogg Blvd.
St. Paul, MN 55101
612-296-7107

Department of Public Welfare
4th floor, Centennial Office Bldg.
St. Paul, MN 55155
612-296-2701

Department of Transportation
Transportation Bldg.
St. Paul, MN 55155
612-296-3131


## FEDERAL OFFICES

Federal Information Center
110 S. 4th St.
Minneapolis, MN 55401
612-725-2073

United States District Court Clerk
316 N. Robert
St. Paul, MN 55101
612-725-7179

Office of the U.S. Attorney
U.S. Courthouse
Room 234
Minneapolis, MN 55401
612-332-8961


## LOCAL LAW-RELATED EDUCATION ORGANIZATIONS

Community Law Center
Hamline University School of Law
Hewitt Ave. & Snelling Ave. N.
St. Paul, MN 55104
612-641-2121

Court Information Office
Minnesota Supreme Court
230 State Capitol
St. Paul, MN 55155
612-296-5096

Minnesota State Bar Association
100 Minnesota Federal Bldg.
Minneapolis, MN 55402
612-335-1183

State Department of Education
Social Studies Instruction
600 Capitol Square Bldg.
550 Cedar St.
St. Paul, MN 55101
612-296-4076

Minnesota Government Training Center
and Urban Concern Project 120
600 Capitol Square Bldg.
550 Cedar St.
St. Paul, MN 55101
612-296-4076


## MINNESOTA COURTS


Supreme Court of Minnesota
230 State Capitol
St. Paul, MN 55155
612-296-2581


## CHIEF DISTRICT COURT JUDGES (Current to 7-1-81)


Hon. Robert J. Breunig
Scott County Courthouse
Shakopee, MN 55379
612-437-3191

Hon. Edward D. Mulally
1521 Ramsey County Courthouse
St. Paul, MN 55102
612-298-4541

Hon. O. Russell Olson
Olmsted County Courthouse
Rochester, MN 55901

Hon. Eugene Minenko
Courts Tower
Government Center
Minneapolis, MN 55487
612-348-2277

Hon. Walter H. Mann
Lyon County Courthouse
Marshall, MN 56258
507-532-5259

Hon. Donald C. Odden
St. Louis County Courthouse
Duluth, MN 55802
218-723-3545

Hon. Paul Hoffman
Stearns County Courthouse
St. Cloud, MN 56301
612-255-6100

Hon. Thomas J. Stahler
Stevens County Courthouse
Morris, MN 56267

Hon. John A. Spellacy
Itasca County Courthouse
Grand Rapids, MN 55744
218-326-3052

Hon. Carroll E. Larson
Wright County Courthouse
Buffalo, MN 55313
612-682-3900 Ext. 145


## DISTRICT COURT ADMINISTRATORS

1st Judicial District:
Esther S. Feldman
Government Center
Hastings, MN 55033
612-437-0330

2nd Judicial District:
Gordon M. Griller
Ramsey County Courthouse
St. Paul, MN 55102

3rd Judicial District:
Donald Cullen
401 N. Main St., Suite 202
Austin, MN 55912
507-437-7741

4th Judicial District:
Jack M. Provo
Courts Tower
Government Center
Minneapolis, MN 55487
612-348-5015

5th Judicial District:
Gerald J. Winter
Box 397 - Courthouse
St. James, MN 56081
507-375-3341 Ext. 218
612-296-0759

6th Judicial District:
Stuart A. Beck
425 Courthouse
Duluth, MN 55802
218-723-3709

7th Judicial District:
James P. Siette
Clay County Courthouse
Moorhead, MN 56560
218-233-2781 Ext. 314

8th Judicial District:
A. Milton Johnson
Chippewa County Courthouse
Montevideo, MN 56265
612-269-7990

9th Judicial District:
Dennis E. Howard
Beltrami County Courthouse
Bemidji, MN 56601
218-751-7300 Ext. 167 & 168

10th Judicial District:
F. Dale Kasparek, Jr.
Anoka County Courthouse
Anoka, MN 55303
612-421-4760 Ext. 1180


County Attorney Council
40 N. Milton
St. Paul, MN 55104
612-296-6972

State Public Defender's Office
The Law School
University of Minnesota
Minneapolis, MN 55455
612-373-5725

# INDEX